P9-CJN-479

THE TRANSVESTITE MEMOIRS OF
THE ABBÉ DE CHOISY

BY THE SAME AUTHOR
Jean-Baptiste Lully

THE TRANSVESTITE MEMOIRS OF

The Abbé de Choisy

AND THE STORY OF
THE MARQUISE-MARQUIS DE BANNEVILLE

Translated from the French
and with an Introduction by

R. H. F. SCOTT

PETER OWEN · LONDON

ISBN 0 7206 0053 7

PETER OWEN LIMITED
20 Holland Park Avenue London W11 3QU

First British Commonwealth edition 1973
© R. H. F. Scott 1973

Printed in Great Britain by
Daedalus Press Stoke Ferry King's Lynn Norfolk

CONTENTS

ILLUSTRATIONS

Illustrations 1 and 2 are reproduced by courtesy of
Radio Times Hulton Picture Library, London, 3 and 4
by courtesy of the Victoria and Albert Museum, London
(Crown Copyright).

Part One

INTRODUCTION

The abbé de Choisy (1644 to 1724), courtier, diarist, historian and transvestite, was an unusual if not bizarre character. He is best known for his *Mémoires pour servir à l'histoire de Louis XIV*, and for the transvestite *Fragments* which form the first part of this volume. Part Two, the 'Story of the Marquise-Marquis de Banneville' is a transvestite tale for which Choisy is thought to have been partly responsible and has its own Introduction.

We learn much about the French Court in the seventeenth and early eighteenth centuries from the abbé de Choisy's vivid and witty memoirs, for he cultivated a wide circle of friends among the nobility and often attended Court, to which his grandfather had obtained entrée during the reign of Henri III.

Choisy *grandpère* was one of the twenty *marchands de vin* attached to the court of Henri III. He arrived at Meulan at the same time and at the same hostelry as the Marquis d'O, then *surintendant des finances*.[1] They played chess together and the Marquis was diplomatically allowed to win. This fortuitous meeting resulted in the loser's promotion to the position of *conseiller d'état*,[2] which he held under Henri III and Henri IV. He married Magdelaine Le Charron d'Ormelles, a lady from the *noblesse de robe*,[3] and died when he was ninety. His son Jean, born in 1598, benefited from his father's success, becoming *maître des requêtes*[4] when he was only twenty-four. Six years later he married Jeanne Olympe de Belesbat, a young woman well versed in court intrigues, who exercised her influence to bring about his appointment as *conseiller d'état* and later as Chancellor to Gaston d'Orleans, Louis XIII's brother.

As *intendant*[5] of Languedoc, Jean de Choisy was ordered to

11

arrest Louis XIII's fallen favourite, Cinq-Mars, and to seize his papers. Finding him burning a pile of letters, Choisy allowed him to continue, whereupon Cinq-Mars turned to his captor with the words, 'You were right, Monsieur, for you would have been most troubled to discover what I have just burnt.' They were love letters from Marie de Gonzagues, later to become Queen of Poland, and also from Choisy's wife, Jeanne Olympe.

Jeanne Olympe was the eldest daughter of Monsieur de Belesbat of the House of Hurault. Her mother was the only daughter of Michel de l'Hospital, an austere and scholarly Chancellor who was a notable administrator. Mademoiselle de Montpensier, the cousin of Louis XIV, wrote in her *Mémoires* of Jeanne Olympe: *Quoique j'aie toujours traité madame de Choisy de folle, je n'ai pas laissé de l'écouter, parce qu'elle voyait beaucoup de monde et qu'elle savait bien des nouvelles.* Devoted as she was to the Court and its intrigues, Jeanne Olympe was even more attentive to Louis XIV: she realized instinctively that even when Mazarin and, after him, Fouquet, seemed to be the most powerful men in the country, the ultimate authority lay with the King. When Gaston d'Orleans and Jean de Choisy died in quick succession in 1660, she was dependent upon royal patronage. Fortunately she was successful in this, obtaining pensions of 6000 livres from Marie de Gonzagues and 8000 livres from Louis himself. Louis evidently liked and respected her. She had once told him that if he wanted to become *un honnête homme* he should converse with her often and he had taken her advice, seeing her twice a week. *Honnête homme* had a particular meaning at that time: Desnoiresterres, writing in the nineteenth century, quoted Bussy-Rabutin: *L'honnête homme est un homme poli et qui sçait vivre,* and then gave his own definition: *Un homme poli façonné aux belles manières et au beau langage, à la grande et noble galanterie des précieuses;* [6] in other words, a perfect courtier. Jeanne Olympe was a *précieuse* herself in the early years before the word and all it stood for were ridiculed by Molière.

She already had three sons and was in her forties when she gave birth to François Timoléon, the future abbé de Choisy, on 16 August, 1644. Delighted as she was to have borne a child in her middle age, she nevertheless brought him up in a most extraordinary way. That her husband permitted her to do so is evidence of the strength of her personality. The child was raised as if he were a girl : his ears were pierced, he wore patches and he had a depilatory lotion applied to his face. He was in constant attendance on his mother in her bedroom and was often dressed in girls' clothes, invariably so when Monsieur, the King's homosexual and transvestite brother, came to pay a visit. The boy apparently enjoyed this imposed transvestism for, after his mother's death, he continued to wear female clothes and successfully passed himself off as a young woman, as recounted in the ensuing text.

His mother encouraged him to meet only the *noblesse d'épée*. These were families whose forebears had been granted titles in medieval times in return for military service to the King. 'Listen, my son,' Jeanne Olympe told him, 'do not be presumptuous but accept the fact that you are only a bourgeois. I know that your father and grandfather were *maîtres des requêtes, conseillers d'état*, but you may take it from me that in France no nobility is recognized except that of the *épée*. Our warrior nation has always looked to the army for its glory. So, my son, mix only with people of quality and avoid presumption. Pass your afternoons with the children of Lesdiguieres, the Marquis de Villeroy, the Comte de Guiche, Louvigny; you will soon be accustomed to good manners and you will have, for the rest of your life, an air of civility which will make everyone like you.' Choisy was made to follow this advice. He never mixed with the administrative officials and was forced to pass his time either at Court with his friends or in his study with his books.

In his memoirs he gives an example of his mother's firmness about his choice of friends. The Duc d'Albret and the abbé d'Harcourt, both contemporaries of his, had quarrelled. The next

13

day his mother asked him if he had seen d'Albret; he replied that he had not, since the abbé d'Harcourt was his friend. His mother looked as if she could devour him. 'What!' she cried, 'Turenne's nephew! Go at once to him or get out of this house.' Madame de Choisy's rage can be explained by the fact that Turenne was not only a close friend of hers but a man of power and influence : d'Albret, the nephew, was made a cardinal when he was only twenty-five. The outcome of this incident was a lasting friendship with the Duc d'Albret; Choisy was loyal to him years later when, as Cardinal de Bouillon, he was exiled by Louis XIV in 1686.

At the age of eighteen Choisy attended the Sorbonne for his *tentative*. [7] He was intelligent but ill-prepared for the examination. However, a friend at Court, Pérefixe, the Archbishop of Paris, told him in advance the three arguments he would have to expound and warned him that he would have to contend with a quibbling casuist, the abbé de Tellier (later Archbishop of Paris) who would try to get the better of him through his eloquence and would force the President of the Examiners to make an unfavourable pronouncement. Pérefixe, who was to be President, gave Choisy his word that he would not utter a syllable. When it came to the examination, Choisy's tactics were successful : whenever Tellier appealed to the examining board, Choisy outshouted him. The vociferous slanging match became unendurable, gavels were rapped, they were both told to be quiet and Choisy passed. Through his mother's influence he was shortly afterwards given the abbacy of Saint Seine.

He may at this time have left Paris to spend five months at Bordeaux where he appeared on the stage as a woman and had male suitors : he mentions this episode briefly in the text. When he was twenty-two his mother died, and he gave himself wholly to transvestism, being accepted as a false young noblewoman in Paris and as a real one in a village near Bourges. By that time his conduct had become intolerable to his relatives who remonstrated with him so forcibly that he left France for Italy, where he remained until he had lost all his money through gambling, to which he was addicted. Destitute by his own standards, he returned to France to live on his benefices which, although inadequate to support his extravagant taste in women's clothes and his gourmét's passion, were otherwise rich enough, bringing him 14000 livres a year. He went to live at his abbey at Saint Seine, near Dijon, and there met Bussy-Rabutin, a somewhat scandalous person who had at one time abducted Choisy's cousin, Madame de Miramion. At this period Bussy-Rabutin was exiled to his estates for having published his *Histoire Amoureuse des Gaulles* in which he had written scabrously about the ladies of the Court. He was insufferably arrogant and conceited which Choisy, though vain, was not, but he was intelligent and the two men became friends in exile. Bussy-Rabutin implanted in Choisy's mind the idea of writing popular and intelligible books on ecclesiastical subjects.

At Dijon Choisy also met a pretty young coquette who immediately took his fancy. She was a Madame Bossuet, married to the *trésorier général*[8] of Burgundy whose brother was Jacques-Bénigne Bossuet, then Bishop of Condom and tutor to the Dauphin. Choisy and Madame Bossuet had an affair but it is uncertain how serious it was. Bussy-Rabutin, after Choisy's return to Paris, acted as intermediary for their correspondence.

Choisy returned to Paris, still in somewhat low water, and sought the favour of his childhood friend d'Albret, who was by then Cardinal de Bouillon. He was not ignored and was invited to accompany the Cardinal as part of his suite on some of Louis XIV's campaigns, in particular that of the Passage of the Rhine in 1672 where, no priests being available, he and the abbé de Dangeau served Mass to the King. Dangeau later converted Choisy to a fervent belief in Catholicism and Choisy remained devoted to him. One anecdote of Choisy's on the Passage of the Rhine is worth quoting:

15

[The King made a mistake] in not swimming the Rhine after the Comte de Guiche, at the head of his *gardes du corps*. There was little risk for him to run and there was infinite *gloire* to be seized....It is true that we must do him justice; he wanted to, but monsieur le Prince [Condé], who dared not set foot to earth because of his gout, opposed it. How could he cross in a boat when the King swam? I was a witness, I was present.

During this period Choisy visited England. He mentions this not only in his transvestite memoirs but also in his account of his voyage to Siam, where he contrasts his terror at crossing the Channel with his serene confidence at the prospect of sailing across the world. How long he was in England and what he did there is regrettably not known.

Pope Clement X died in 1676. Four French cardinals were sent to Rome to assist in the election of the new Pope; Choisy accompanied Cardinal de Bouillon as *conclaviste*. [9] He was so tactful and efficient that, through the influence of Cardinal de Retz, he became *conclaviste* to the French delegation. He related that he was the first to kiss the feet of the new Pope, Innocent XI, formerly Cardinal Odescalchi, a Milanese. The French cardinals, using Choisy's persuasive pen for writing despatches, had persuaded Louis that Odescalchi was the right choice for France. In the event he was by no means favourable to French interests and, according to d'Alembert, Grimaldi, one of the French Cardinals, had no high opinion of him: at the ceremony of adoration of the new Pope, Grimaldi approached him and said in a voice loud enough to be heard only by those nearby: 'Remember that you are ignorant and bigoted; that is the last time you will hear the truth from me; now I am going to adore you.'

In 1683 Choisy fell gravely ill and thought he was dying, an opinion reinforced by his physicians. He had delirious visions of a hell populated by ne're-do-wells dressed as women and of *conclavistes* who were sceptics. He was so alarmed that he resolved to live devoutly if he recovered. He did recover and, to his credit, did not renegue: he not only became a true believer but developed into a church historian, if not a theologian. His conversion, as has been mentioned, was undertaken by his old friend Dangeau. Dangeau had also led a dissolute life and had himself been converted from Protestantism by Bossuet. The conversion of Choisy was published in the form of dialogues between Théophile (Dangeau) and Timoléon (Choisy), the immortality of the soul being demonstrated by such unusual analogies as Poussin's paintings, Talbot's soup, and the singing of Mademoiselle Rochouas (sic – presumably Le Rochois, the leading soprano at the Opéra). Choisy was altogether too easy an opponent for Dangeau who remarked: 'I had scarcely proved the existence of God to this scatterbrain when I saw him ready to believe in the baptism of bells.' Choisy, on the other hand, maintained a great respect and affection for Dangeau, which is manifest in his *Voyage to Siam*.

When Choisy was restored to health he went to a seminary for Missions to Foreigners and there learnt that an embassy was to be sent to Siam in acknowledgement of one from that country, the members of which were still in Paris. He applied to be the Ambassador and, having enlisted the powerful support of the Cardinal de Bouillon, might have been granted the appointment, although it is difficult to believe that Louis XIV, who knew him well, would have put in charge of this important undertaking a man who, though genial, was so completely lacking in *gravitas*. His application was, in any case, too late: the Chevalier de Chaumont had already been chosen. Undeterred, Choisy argued that the Ambassador could easily die en route and that it would be prudent for a deputy to travel with him. He pleaded his case so well that the King was convinced and Choisy was made coadjutor to the Ambassador with the task of converting, if possible, the King of Siam to Christianity. The King commented: 'I have never heard of a coadjutor to an embassy. But he is right, because of the length and danger of such a journey.'

Choisy accordingly left with the embassy in 1685, was made a priest in four days by the Bishop *in partibus* in Siam, and returned, imperturbably cheerful as ever, in 1686. A manuscript note to the 1727 edition of Choisy's *Mémoires pour servir à l'histoire de Louis XIV* states that, before leaving France he married a Mlle de Gardebelé, who bore him a child : this gave rise to his being called *mari sur terre et prestre sur mer*.

The safe return of the embassy caused much excitement and Choisy, with the others, was fêted at Court. They had brought with them a second embassy from Siam and a great number of presents from the Siamese Royal family to the French Royal family. Choisy had also seen to it that there were presents for his friend, the Cardinal de Bouillon. Unfortunately, while Choisy was away, the Cardinal had incurred the King's displeasure and was in exile in Tarascon. Choisy, when he learnt this, hoped that no inkling of the Cardinal's presents would reach the King's ear, but when he overheard some courtiers talking about them he asked for an audience with Louis, who granted it with *un visage solaire*. After Choisy had confessed his quite understandable error of judgement, the *visage* was no longer *solaire* and the King dismissed him with a look calculated to put him a hundred feet under the earth. Choisy fled to an inn where he hid himself for the rest of the day. The royal rage remaining unabated, he left the next day for his seminary in Paris, where half an hour's prayer before the Holy Sacrament restored his composure. The King's irritability can be partly explained by the pain he was suffering from a fistula, which had been aggravated by the remedial treatment given to him.

The following year was happier for Choisy. During his absence from France he had kept a diary in the form of letters to the abbé de Dangeau. This was published in 1687 as *Journal ou suite du voyage de Siam* and achieved an immediate and merited success. St Evremond spoke well of it and later Sainte-Beuve praised it highly. It is still regarded as a minor classic in France because Choisy wrote excellent French. The *Journal* makes decidedly entertaining reading, Choisy having a quick eye for amusing trivialities even on solemn occasions, and a good descriptive style. He then published his *Vie de David* which was patently an allegorical glorification of Louis. He followed this with a critical examination of the Psalms, in which he noted differences between the Vulgate translation and the original Hebrew. Through the intercession of Père de la Chaise, the King's Confessor, he presented copies of both these works to the King, who graciously accepted them. His *Vie de Salomon* which came out a little later, was again a transparent eulogy of Louis. His success with the *Journal de Siam* coincided with a vacancy in the Académie française, to which he was admitted in 1687.

Between 1688 and 1695 he wrote *Histoire de Philippe de Valois et du Rois Jean, Histoire de Charles V, Histoire de Charles VI* and, in three weeks, the *Vie de Saint Louis* (Louis IX). While he was working on the life of Charles VI, he was approached by the Dauphin's eldest son, the Duc de Bourgogne. The boy was evidently shocked at the idea that his grandfather's infirmity should be revealed in the book. Believing that monarchs should remain beyond criticism, no matter how long they had been dead, he asked Choisy how he would contrive to convey the fact that Charles VI had been mad. 'Monseigneur,' Choisy replied, 'I shall say that he was mad.' He was immensely proud of this reply, comparing it with that of Mézeray, a French historian who had died in 1683, to Louis XIV. Louis had asked why he had described Louis XI as a tyrant, to which Mézeray replied, 'Why, was he one?' Choisy's repartee was admired by others, too. Even the Duc de Montausier, a grim old soldier who had once humiliated Choisy by ejecting him from the young Dauphin's box at the Opéra because he was in full woman's evening dress, conceded that it was commendable. 'It annoys me', he said, 'not to be able to give this hermaphrodite a sign of friendship.'

Choisy always enjoyed company and, even by English nineteenth-century standards, he would have been a clubbable man despite his eccentricities. He formed a kind of club himself, a literary association of thirteen members, mostly Academicians, who met at his lodgings in the Palais du Luxembourg. It included Dangeau, Caumartin, Perrault and Fontanelle. Because they discussed politics and moral philosophy as well as literature they were enjoined to keep their meetings confidential. Nevertheless, the club incurred official displeasure and was short-lived. A similar association called *le Club de l'Entresol* was formed in 1724, the year of Choisy's death.

At one meeting of Choisy's select coterie there was a discussion about what title should be given to his Imitation of Christ, on which he was working. After some debate no better title could be found than *Imitation de Jésus-Christ,* and in due course it was published under that name. It was an immediate best-seller, not because of the unexceptionable text but because of one of the illustrations. This was a crude engraving of Madame de Maintenon kneeling before a crucifix. The scandal concerned the caption which ran *Audi, filia* and was quickly traced to the forty-fourth psalm of the Vulgate : *Audi filia, inclina aurem tuam, et oblivescere domum patris tui. Et concupiscet rex decorem tuam.* Madame de Maintenon had been the King's mistress for some time and, it is generally believed, had been privately married to him in 1683. As a warning, therefore, it was too late but Choisy must have known this and he was too accomplished a courtier to have offended the King knowingly. It was a simple, unintentional gaffe, but the infamous illustration was not removed until the fourth edition.

Choisy's most monumental work was his *History of the Church* which he undertook at the instigation of Bossuet. It consisted of eleven quarto volumes, the production of which took him from 1703 to 1723. It is said that when he had completed it, he remarked : 'Thanks to God I have finished the *History of the Church,* and I am now going to get down to studying the subject.'

His *Mémoires pour servir à l'histoire de Louis XIV* are easy to read and worth doing so for his descriptions of seventeenth-century notables. Sainte-Beuve praised two in particular, those of Colbert and Louise de la Vallière, who was a childhood friend of Choisy. He also commented favourably upon Choisy's felicitous style, which is light and intimate, as if he were conducting an amusing private chat with the reader. Indeed, he himself says in the *Mémoires* that he 'chattered when he had a pen in his hand'. He avoids verbosity completely and his descriptions are vivid and sometimes startlingly modern, as when, in the *Voyage de Siam*, he describes a baby as *un petit éléphant de poche*. He is good-humoured and irrepressible; even when he is cast down through having, for example, incurred the King's displeasure, he soon bobs up again with unimpaired serenity. One apt comment on the *Mémoires* is a manuscript note of Clairambault's at the end of the Preface to the Utrecht edition of 1727 :

> Choisi n'est icy qu'ébauché :
> Sa vie on devrait bien écrire.
> Mais jamais on ne pourra dire
> S'il fut plus fou que débauché.

Choisy also wrote one novel, *La Nouvelle Astrée*, a pastoral romance of no great interest except that it, inevitably, involves a young shepherd dressed as a woman, besides (probably) *La Marquise-Marquis de Banneville*, already mentioned.[10]

In time Choisy became Prior of St Lô de Rouen, of St Benoît de Sault near Bourges and of St Gelais. He had been dismissed from his abbacy of St Seine in 1676, but it is not known why. At the end of the century his surviving brother died and he inherited the family château of Balleroy in the Dauphiné, one of Mansart's first buildings. Although he had to sell it to pay the debts he had incurred mostly through gambling, his passion for it never left him. His insatiable yearning to dress as a woman continued also, even though in later years he could not afford the elaborate dresses and ornaments he had affected in his youth. When he could not play cards for cash he played for credit, and there is an anecdote, of dubious authenticity but certainly in character, which relates that he lost fifty louis to Madame Dufresnoy and did not pay her; eventually she wrote to him asking for the

money and in reply he sent her a copy of his works with a covering note saying that they would help her to kill the time until he
was ready to settle his debt with her.

Choisy continued to write, to gamble, to be genially sociable
and to dress as a woman *dans les Compagnies et même à l'Eglise*
until he died in 1724.

The Transvestite Memoirs

The *Fragments* which compose the following text were filched,
together with the *Mémoires*, from Choisy's executor and kinsman,
the Marquis d'Argenson. This somewhat proper man, after men-
tioning that the conversation of old men was instructive if one
pumped them enough, wrote in his own *Mémoires*:

> That was the way I treated my kinsman, the abbé de Choisy,
> with whom I lived in the last years of his life. I must admit,
> in spite of the affection he had for me, that he was by no means
> a worthy man. He was a weak soul and had more feeling for
> society than for good conduct. But he came to be received into
> the Académie and to earn some sort of reputation in that com-
> pany because he wrote and spoke well.
>
> Moreover he was not fitted to become a bishop nor to be
> employed in any important affair; he was always conscious of
> his effeminate upbringing, and, when he was past the age of
> dressing as a woman, was never able to think as a man. In spite
> of all his faults, and he was very old when I knew him, he was
> marvellous to hear. His memory was full of anecdotes about
> the Court, which he had frequented, though he never played
> an important part there, and in which he had lived so long. He
> also had the flair for discerning the worth of a characteristic or
> a witticism.

D'Argenson described how the manuscripts left his hands and
were published without his knowledge:

> He handed over all his manuscripts to me shortly before he
> died and I extracted what I thought the most interesting and

22

made three large volumes of them. I could hardly refuse the request of a lady belonging to the family who was curious to read them. She kept them a long time and let the abbé d'Olivet have access to them. He produced a work of two small volumes under the title of *Mémoires pour servir à l'histoire de Louis XIV by the late abbé de Choisy*. It is certain that these two volumes contained the cream, if one may so express it, of the manuscripts entrusted to me. . . .

One of the manuscripts which he left me contained the story of himself as the Comtesse des Barres. In my manuscript there were five volumes and only three have been published; but I believe that the rest will appear, for the same person who had allowed the *Mémoires* to be published had given out copies of that fragment.

D'Argenson's opinion of the 'fragment' is interesting :

When reading it, everyone finds it very well written, containing some erotic passages scarcely edifying but most readable. At the same time the story is regarded as quite unbelievable. I can, however, guarantee that it is quite true. The old abbé, long after he wrote the Lives of David and Solomon and his instructive histories, such as that of the church, would often tell me of his misspent youth with unspeakable delight, and I would stare in amazement at this man whose life had been so full of strange incongruities.

That is enough of this work which does no honour to my old friend and kinsman.

To remark on one of the occasions when the abbé de Choisy figured as an Academician, let us say that in the last years of his life he received the abbé d'Olivet. His speech was brief and simple. The poor man was on his last legs but he insisted on this duty because the abbé d'Olivet was his friend. I do not know if it was for that reason that he filched the *Mémoires* from me and took it on himself to have them printed in Holland.

23

Paul Lacroix, in his Preface to the first complete edition of the *Fragments* in 1862, quoted another comment by d'Argenson: He said:

The Bibliothêque de l'Arsenal has a most curious collection of manuscripts, often quoted but so far only published in part: *Ouvrages de M. l'abbé de Choisy, qui n'ont pas été imprimés.* This collection comprises three quarto volumes. . . . At the head of the first volume is an autograph note by the Marquis d'Argenson: 'These works by the abbé de Choisy were delivered to me after his death and were taken from a quantity of useless papers which he had neglected. I arranged them in order in a way which seemed suitable to me. My intention was that they should not leave my study. But among many to whom I could not refuse a reading there were some who, without my knowledge, took it on themselves to make public the Memoirs of which this is the original. The abbé d'Olivet, his friend, believes that the author had finished his Memoirs on Louis XIV, and that a year before he died he had burnt what is lacking here. These Memoirs are in the first volume.

The first volume contained various memoirs, some of which were added to the *Mémoires pour servir* etc. which comprised the second volume, when they were published. The third volume was the *Cinq fragments de la vie de cet ecclésiastique habillé en femme.*

Before Lacroix's edition only the Comtesse des Barres episode had been published and that in a corrupt text. Another complete edition was published in 1920, limited to 1000 copies in a series entitled *Le Livre du Boudoir,* by the Bibliothêque des Curieux, with an introduction by the *Chevalier de Percefleur, Membre Correspondant de l'Académie des Dames.* 'Le Chevalier de Perce-fleur' might be translated as 'Sir Pluck Cherry'; the *Académie des Dames* was an eighteenth-century pornographic book.

The first sentence of the *Fragments* is *Vous m'ordonnez, Madame, d'écrire l'histoire de ma vie,* and occasionally later in

24

the text there is an address to *Madame*. This was the Marquise de Lambert (1647-1733), a high-spirited woman who wrote works of moral instruction such as *Avis d'une mére à son fils* and *Avis à sa fille* and whose salon, held twice a week until she died, was famous for its aristocracy and literary habitués. That she encouraged Choisy to write of his deplorable youth, the details of which she must have known, shows that the moral tone of her books evidently did not preclude her liking for racy gossip.

The *Fragments* are somewhat confusing, both chronologically and with regard to historical detail, rich though they are in information about the costume and customs of the time. The last fragment, the Comtesse des Barres episode, gives details of his mother's death and the apportioning of her estate, after which Choisy gave reign to his transvestism. Nevertheless it is not chronologically first since, quite apart from the clearly exordial opening sentence of the first fragment, he refers early in the fourth to his being called 'Madame de Sancy' which is the subject of the first fragment. If one were editing, the first and second fragments would be interpolated there. The placing of the third fragment is explained in the Notes, though both it and the fourth end with Choisy's departure for Italy. As Desnoiresterres wrote in exasperation : *Choisy nous embarrasse à tout instant par l'impossibilité de coordonner ses différents récits.*

Choisy was in his late sixties or early seventies when he wrote his memoirs, so he can perhaps be forgiven for this inexactitude, and for certain anachronisms and discrepancies in the *Fragments*. These are numbered in the text as they occur and explained in the corresponding Notes following Part Two, together with explanations of Choisy's lovingly-described costumes.

As to the content of Choisy's memoirs, we should read his bizarre sexual exploits against the background of late seventeenth-century French court life. It was, for example, the custom for a lady to hold a salon in her bedroom, and for a visitor to share the host or hostess's bed. Choisy's curious delight in making love in front of mixed company without its being perceived was evidently an extension of his almost boundless vanity. He blamed, as has always been the custom, his upbringing for his weaknesses and peculiar tastes, but was quite without regret. He is often almost emetically unattractive – there is something not only ludicrous but odious in the idea of a man fornicating in curl-papers – but there are more forgivable aspects of his behaviour. It was he who ran a household perfectly, he who gave others good practical advice and he who came to the rescue of a recital in jeopardy by faultlessly accompanying the quartet on a harpsichord. A man of intelligence, he is saved from appearing completely repellent by his good nature and his invincible naïvety.

THE TRANSVESTITE MEMOIRS

I

The first affairs of the abbé de Choisy
under the name of Madame de Sancy

You have ordered me, Madame, to write the story of my life; in truth, you cannot imagine it. I assure you that you will read neither of towns taken nor of battles won; politics will be no more conspicuous than war. Do not expect anything other than bagatelles, little pleasures and childish amusements. A fairly happy disposition, gentle affections, no black dog on the shoulder, everywhere delight, a desire to please, lively passions: these are defects in a man but virtues in the fair sex. If you are ashamed when you read, what shall I be when I write? To look for excuses in my ill-conceived upbringing would be pointless, no-one would accept them. That is enough of useless preambles; you command, and I obey. But I ask you to approve, Madame, that I obey you only in part; I shall write of one or two acts of my comedy which will have no bearing on the rest. For example, I have a great desire to recount to you the great and memorable adventures in the fauborg Saint-Marceau.

A habit acquired in infancy is strange, it is impossible to overcome it: my mother, almost from my birth, accustomed me to women's garments and I continued to wear them in my youth. I have taken the part of a girl for five months in the theatre of a large town; everyone was deceived. I had admirers to whom I allowed some little favours, but was strict about anything more; my modest behaviour was common knowledge. I had the most delightful time that anyone can experience in this life.

Gambling, which has always been my downfall, cured me of these minor frivolities for several years, but every time that I was ruined and wanted to cease gambling, I fell, yielded to my old weaknesses and became a woman again.

I bought, for this purpose, a house in the faubourg Saint-Marceau, where both the bourgeoisie and the common people lived, so that I could dress myself as I pleased among people who would not take exception to what I did. I began by having my ears pierced again, the holes from earlier piercing having closed up. I wore embroidered corsets and gold and black *robes de chambre,*[11] with sleeves lined with white satin, a girdle with a busk and a large knot of ribbons behind to mark the waist, a wide trailing train, a well-powdered peruke, ear pendants, patches[12] and a cap with a *fontange.*[13]

At first I had only a *robe de chambre* of black cloth, fastened in front with black buttons which went down to the lowest edge, a long train which a lackey held, a small peruke lightly powdered, quite simple earrings, and two large velvet patches at the temples. I went to see the curé of Saint-Médard, who warmly praised my attire, and told me that it was far more becoming than that of all the little abbés with their *just-au-corps*[14] and little cloaks which commanded no respect; that was until quite recently the dress of many curés in Paris. Afterwards I went to see the churchwardens from whom I had rented a pew opposite the pulpit, and then I made calls on everyone in the district, the Marquise d'Usson, the Marquise de Menières, and all my other female neighbours. I wore no other dress for a month, and I never missed High Mass on Sundays nor the curé's sermons, which pleased him greatly. Once a week I went with the curé or Monsieur Garnier, whom I had chosen as my confessor, to visit the poor and distressed, and to distribute charity. But, at the end of a month, I undid three or four buttons at the top of my robe so that my bodice of silver moiré,[15] which I wore underneath, could be seen. I put on my diamond earrings, which I had bought five or six years beforehand from Monsieur Lambert, the jeweller. My peruke became a little longer and more powdered, cut in such a way that my earrings were in full view, and I put on three or four little patches around my mouth or on my forehead. I remained like this for a month, so that people would, without their knowing it, become accustomed to my apparel, and would believe that I had always been the same; and that is what happened. As soon as I saw that my plan had succeeded, I opened five or six buttonholes at the bottom of my gown, in order to reveal a robe of speckled black satin, the train of which was not as long as the gown. I also wore a white damask underskirt, which could be seen only when the train was carried. I ceased to wear trunk-hose; to me it was hardly becoming to a woman and I had no fear of being cold, because it was full summer. I had a muslin cravat, whose tassels dropped on a huge knot of black ribbon which was attached to the top of my *robe de chambre*. The gown revealed my shoulders which always remained quite white through the great care I had taken of them all my life: every evening I laved my neck with veal water and sheep's-foot grease, which made the skin soft and white.

So, by degrees, I accustomed people to seeing me dressed up in this way. I was giving supper to Madame d'Usson and five or six of my lady neighbours, when the curé called to see me at seven in the evening. We invited him to sup with us and he, a fine man, stayed.

'From now on,' Madame d'Usson said to me, 'I shall call you "Madame".' She turned me round before the curé, saying to him : 'Is not that a lovely woman?'

'That is true,' he said, 'but she is in masquerade.'

'No monsieur,' I said to him, 'no; in the future I shall not dress otherwise. I shall wear only black gowns lined with white, or white gowns lined with black; no one will be able to fault me. These ladies, as you can see, advised me on this confection; they

29

assure me that it is not unbecoming. Moreover, I tell you that I supped, two days ago, with Madame the Marquise de Noailles; Monsieur, her brother-in-law, called there and warmly praised my costume, and in his presence all the company called me "Madame".'

'Ah!' said the curé, 'I must yield to such an authority, and I do acknowledge, madame, that you look very fine.'

Supper was announced; we remained at table until eleven o'clock, and my servants escorted the curé home.

After that time I went to see him and had no more scruples about going everywhere in a *robe de chambre,* and everyone became used to it.

I have considered carefully whence came such a bizarre taste and here is my explanation : the attribute of God is to be loved, adored; Man, as far as the weakness of his nature allows, wishes for the same but, as it is beauty that kindles love and since that is usually the lot of women, when it happens that men have, or believe themselves to have, certain traits of beauty, they try to enhance them by the same methods that women use, which are most becoming. They feel the inexpressible pleasure of being loved. I have felt this more than once during a delightful affair. When I was at a ball or the theatre, wearing my beautiful *robes de chambre,* diamonds and patches, and heard people murmur near me 'There is a lovely woman', I experienced an inward glow of pleasure which is incomparable, it is so strong. Ambition, riches, even love do not equal it, because we always love ourselves more deeply than we love others.

From time to time I gave supper to my lady neighbours. I made no pretence of giving feasts. I usually chose Sundays and holidays as the bourgeois are always more presentable on those days and have nothing to do except enjoy themselves.

One day when I had as my guests Madame Dupuis and her two daughters, Monsieur Renard, his wife, his grand-daughter Mademoiselle Charlotte and his grandson Monsieur de la Neuville, at six o'clock in the evening we were in my library. It was well illuminated with a crystal lustre, many mirrors, marble tables, pictures and porcelain : the place was magnificent. I was well apparelled on that day : I had a gown of white damask lined with black taffeta, the train half an ell long; a bodice of heavy silver moiré which could be seen in entirety, a big knot of black ribbon at the top of the bodice, over which hung a muslin cravat with tassels; a skirt of black velvet, whose train was not so long as that of the gown; and two white underskirts which no one could see – they were to prevent my being cold, because since I wore skirts and thus no longer used trunk-hose, I felt truly a woman. On that day I had my lovely earrings of brilliants, a well powdered peruke and more than a dozen patches. The curé came to pay me a visit; everyone was pleased to see him; he was much liked in the parish.

'Ah! madame,' he said to me on entering, 'you are well bedecked. Are you going to a ball?'

'No, monsieur,' I replied, 'but I am giving supper to my lovely neighbours, and I am happy to please them.'

We sat down and talked of the latest news (the curé liked this). Always on my table were copies of the *Gazette,* the *Journal des Savants,* the *Trévaux* and the *Mercure Galant,* and each took the one he liked best. I made him read a little story from the previous month's *Mercure* [16] where it spoke of a man of quality who wished to be a woman because of his beauty, who was delighted to be called 'madame', and who wore fine golden gowns, skirts, ear pendants and patches, and had suitors.

'I can see', I said to them, 'that that is like me, but I do not know whether I should be angry.'

'Ah! why, madame,' said Madame Dupuis, 'why be so angry? Is it not true? Moreover, does it say anything bad about you? On the contrary, it says that you are beautiful. For my part I wish that he had simply mentioned your name, so that everyone would speak more of you, and I have a mind to go and find him and give him that opinion.'

'Take care you do not,' said I, 'I wish to be beautiful in your company, but I go into the town dressed like this as rarely as possible. The world is so wicked, and it is so uncommon to see a man wishing to be a woman that one is often exposed to distasteful pleasantries.'

'What are you saying now, madame?' interrupted the curé. 'Have you ever met anyone who has condemned your conduct in that respect?'

'Yes, indeed, monsieur, I have! I had an uncle,[17] a *conseiller d'état* named Monsieur ——, who, knowing that I dressed myself as a woman, came one morning to give me a good scolding. I was at my *toilette* and had just taken up my shift; I stood up. "No," he said, "sit down and dress yourself." So saying, he sat down opposite me. "Since you command me, dear Uncle," I said, "I shall obey you. It is eleven o'clock and I must go to Mass." My servants dressed me in a bodice laced behind, then a black, cut velvet gown, a skirt of the same material over an ordinary petticoat, a muslin cravat and a gold and black steenkirk.[18] Until then I had kept on my cornets;[19] I now put on a peruke which was well curled and powdered. My good uncle did not say a word. "It will soon be done, dear Uncle," I said. "I have to put on my ear pendants and five or six patches," which I did in a moment. "From what I have seen," he said, "I must now call you my niece, and, really, you are very pretty." I flung my arms round his neck and kissed him two or three times; he made no reproaches to me, made me use his carriage, and took me to Mass and then to dine with him.'

This little anecdote greatly entertained the company. The curé made a pretence of leaving, but he stayed. We supped well, full of happiness and innocence, and finished with mulled wine. I had, in an aside, asked Mademoiselle Dupuis to suggest that we should all go to the summerhouse in the garden, and I said that I would like this. Monsieur de la Neuville gave me his hand to lead me there; I called for a lackey to hold my trains.

'No, no,' said Mlle Dupuis, 'I want to carry them; maids of honour carry the trains of princesses.'

'But,' I said, 'I am not a princess.'

'Well, madame, you are one this evening and I am your maid of honour.'

'Will you be that only for this evening?' said Monsieur de la Neuville, laughing.

I began to laugh too, and said to Mlle Dupuis with solemnity : 'Since I am a princess, I make you one of my maids of honour; take up the train.'

We went down to the summerhouse, and it was so small that it could hardly contain us. We sat on the sofas which encircled the room and, to please my friends, I told them that I would allow them to salute and kiss me. They came in review order and, certain that the curé did not take his turn because of modesty, I stood up and went to embrace him with all my heart.

I used to have a pew opposite the pulpit : the churchwardens always sent a lighted candle for me to join them in the procession and I followed immediately behind them; a lackey carried my train. On the day of the Blessed Sacrament the procession made a long tour, going as far as the Gobelins; Monsieur de la Neuville gave me his hand and acted as my squire. After five or six months I was given the *chanteau* [20] to provide the bread for consecration. I played my part wonderfully well, but I had no wish for acclaim. The churchwardens told me that the consecrated bread had to be presented by a woman and the collection taken by her, and they flattered themselves that I would be willing to accept this honour. I did not know what I should do until the Marquise d'Usson decided me and told me that she had taken the collection herself, and that it would be warmly appreciated throughout the parish. I needed no more pressing, but prepared myself as if for a grand occasion which would show me off magnificently to the whole populace. I had had made a *robe de chambre* of white damask from China, lined with black taffeta : I had an *échelle* [21] of black ribbons, ribbons on the sleeves and, behind, a large bunch of ribbons to mark the waist. I thought that on this occasion I should wear a skirt of black velvet; it was October, and velvet was seasonable.

Since then I have always worn two skirts, and I have turned back my mantuas [22] with huge knots of ribbons. My coiffure was most elegant: a little bonnet of black taffeta, laden with ribbons, was fastened to a well-powdered peruke. Madame de Noailles had lent me her large ear pendants of brilliants, and on the left of my hair I had five or six ornamental hair pins of diamonds and rubies. I wore three or four big patches, and more than a dozen small ones. I have always had a weakness for patches, and I find that there is nothing more becoming. I also had a steenkirk of Mechlin lace, which appeared to conceal a bosom, so I was well turned out.

I presented the blessed bread, I went to the offertory most gracefully, according to what I was told, and then took the collection. I do not wish to boast, but they had never taken so much money at Saint-Médard. I took the collection in the morning at High Mass, and after dinner at Vespers and at Benediction. I had a squire, Monsieur de la Neuville, a lady's maid who also followed me, and three lackeys, one of whom carried my train.

They were incensed against me for having been somewhat coquettish, because on going through the seats I stopped sometimes while the verger made a way for me, and amused myself by looking in my glass to make adjustments to my ear pendants or my steenkirk, but I only did it at Benediction, and not many people noticed it. I worked hard all day, but I was so delighted at finding myself praised by everyone that I felt no fatigue till I was in bed.

I forgot to say that I collected two hundred and seventy-two livres. There were three young men of good appearance whom I did not know at all, each of whom gave me a louis d'or; I believed that they were strangers. It is certain that a great number of people had come from other parishes, knowing that I would be taking the collection, and I confess that in the evening, for the salut, [23] I was most agreeably flattered. It was night and one

34

could speak more freely; I heard, two or three times, in different parts of the church, people who said :

'But is it really true that that is a man? He is quite right to pass himself off as a woman.'

Then I would go back to them and pretend to ask someone for an offering, so that they would have the pleasure of seeing me. It will be understood that in a strange way this confirmed my delight in being treated like a woman. These praises seemed to me to be truths which had in no way been sought; those people did not know me, and did not compliment me to please me.

The life which I led in my little house in the faubourg Saint-Marceau was pleasant enough. My affairs were healthy : my brother had just died and had left me, with all debts paid, nearly fifty thousand écus; I had much fine furniture, a silver service, some silver gilt, earrings of brilliants, two rings which were easily worth four thousand francs, a waist buckle and some pearl and ruby bracelets.

I had a comfortable establishment : two carriages, one for four people and one for two, four carriage-horses, a coachman and a postilion who also acted as a porter, a chaplain, a *valet de chambre,* whose sister looked after my housekeeping and attended to my dressing, three lackeys, a male cook, a scullery maid and a Savoyard to polish my room.

I often gave supper parties for my lady neighbours, and sometimes for the curé and Monsieur Garnier, and although I did not try to be sumptuous, I gave good entertainment. Sometimes I had concerts. I used to send my carriage for my old friend, Descotaux. I gave little lotteries [24] of bagatelles that had an air of magnificence. I took my lady neighbours to the Opéra and to the Comédie. There was always coffee, tea and chocolate at my house. [25] I had Mass said every day by my chaplain, with an offertory, at half an hour after noon. All the idle women in the neighbourhood never missed this, and as I went to bed very late, I was often woken to be told that the bell was ringing for Mass; then I would quickly put on a *robe de chambre,* a skirt and a taffeta coif [26] to hide my night cornets, and run to hear the service; I did not like to miss it. In short, all was happy in my world, until love came to mar my contentment.

Two young ladies, who were neighbours, showed me much affection and would kiss me quite unaffectedly; but I was not sure which of them would suit me best; I often gave them supper, and they always came early and thought only of helping to dress me up. One would adjust my cap, the other my ear pendants; each pleaded for the great favour of being in charge of patches; these were never placed as they liked and, in altering their positions, the girls would kiss me on the cheek or on the forehead. One day they were so free as to kiss me on the lips in such a tender and pressing way that it became clear that this was a demonstration of more than simply good friendship. I said in a whisper to the one who pleased me most (it was Mademoiselle Charlotte):

'Mademoiselle, should I be happy enough to be loved by you?'

'Ah! madame,' she replied, seizing my hand, 'how could one see you without loving you?'

We soon came to terms; we promised each other inviolable secrecy and fidelity.

'I am not constrained', she said to me one day, 'as I would be with a man; all I see is a lovely woman, and why should I stop myself from loving her? What an advantage women's clothes give you! The heart of a man is there, which has its effect on us, and on the other hand the charms of feminity transport us and quite disarm us.'

I replied with equal tenderness, but although I greatly loved her, I loved myself even more and thought only of being pleasing to all mankind.

Mademoiselle Charlotte and I wrote to each other every day and we saw each other constantly; her bedroom window was opposite mine, the narrow rue de Sainte-Geneviève separating us. Her letters were written with a charming artlessness; I gave her back more than a hundred of them, as I shall recount; by chance I still have two :

How kind you were yesterday evening, madame. I was so happy I wanted a hundred times to kiss you in front of everyone. *Eh bien*! they have said that I love you, but is that not true? I do not want to conceal it and if you do not say it I shall myself. My grand-papa said to me in a whisper: 'My girl, I think that Madame de Sancy loves you : you should be very happy.' Oh! madame! I could not restrain myself and I said to him : 'Grand-papa, we love each other with all our hearts, but madame does not want it known.' Adieu, my step-mother is coming in. (This step-mother tormented her.)

Monsieur, I am truly in despair. I wish I had never met you, my distress, of which you are the cause, has cost me so much. I believe that something of our little affair has been discovered; you yourself are the cause of this : why do you whisper in my ear? I have been spied on for some time. I do not know if I have been seen going to the summerhouse, but I have had some most unpleasant scoldings. When you come, talk to me just the same; do not pretend anything, so that they may think they are mistaken. The Holy Ghost inspired me not to go to your house. I was at Mademoiselle Dupuis's, they looked for me there; after that I was at my aunt's, they came there again; take care not to throw anything through my window. I am in truth, monsieur, quite wretched in my love for you. I am writing this letter in great difficulties; I am never a moment in my room before someone comes to see what I am doing. Do not wait for me at the summerhouse any more. As for me, I do not know if they suspect that you give me letters; when you do give me them, pass them to me only when it is quite safe, so that no one will see it. I confess that I am quite miserable; if only for a little, perhaps I should go away to a convent for three months. What do you say to that? Do not ask me 'have you nothing to give me?' When I have a letter, I shall give it to you when I can find the opportunity.

About that time, there was a wedding feast at the house of a person of quality, attended by my kinswomen and my woman friends. I had dined there and I decided to return there in masquerade after supper as there would certainly be music. I went to my house forthwith, and asked my lovely lady neighbours to supper and afterwards told them to disguise themselves. The young ones could not ask for anything better. I dressed Mademoiselle Charlotte *en garçon*. I had hired a complete man's costume for her, quite neat with a fine peruke. She made a very pretty cavalier. They recognized me from the first because they had often seen me in my gowns; so I had to remove my mask and join the ranks of the ladies sitting at the ball; and the rest of my party remained masked. Charlotte led me to dance; the company admired the minuet which we danced together. The excitement by no means harmed me and I returned to my place with a heightened colour which I did not have before dancing. The mistress of the house, who was not given to praise, came and embraced me, whispering :

'I do declare, my dear girl-cousin, that your clothes suit you well. This evening you are as beautiful as an angel.'

I changed the conversation and called Charlotte, who removed her mask so that one could see her lovable pretty little face.

'There, madame,' I said, 'this is my little lover; is he not pretty?'

It was obvious that it was a girl; she replaced her mask and gave me her hand for us to go. Little Charlotte squired me all the evening, and we loved each other more than ever. She observed this and tenderly said to me :

'Alas, madame! I perceive that you love me more when I wear a *just-au-corps;* I wish I were allowed to wear one always!'

The next day I purchased the costume I had hired for her, which might have been made for her. I had it put in a cupboard with the peruke, the gloves, the cravat and the hat. Once when my neighbours came to see me, by chance the cupboard was opened and the costume was seen; at once they almost threw themselves on it, which was just what I wanted for once again my little girl was dressed in it, and there she was, a handsome boy again.

When they had gone, she wanted to change. I would not hear of it, and told her that I was making her a present of the clothes, also that I would never wear them, and that, for payment, all I asked was that she would wear them whenever my lady neighbours did me the honour of supping with me.

Charlotte's aunt, for she had neither father nor mother, made some fuss, and then gave in, all the other women having protested to her that they would accept the same bargain if ever I wanted it. So I had the delight of often having Charlotte *en garçon* and, as I was *en femme,* it was a veritable marriage.

I had a summerhouse at the end of my garden, and there was a back door by which she would come to see me as often as she could, and we had private signs for our own understanding. When she was in the summerhouse, I would place a peruke on her head so that I could pretend she was a boy; she had no trouble, on her part, in imagining that I was a woman; so, both happy, we had much pleasure.

I had, in the summerhouse, many fine portraits; I suggested to my young women neighbours that they should have their likenesses painted, but on condition that Charlotte was painted *en cavalier.* Her aunt, who was dying to have her portrait painted, consented. I wanted at the same time to have myself painted as a woman, for my little love to look at; I had no conceit, she was more beautiful than I. I summoned Monsieur de Troyes,[27] who painted us in the summerhouse; this took him a month, and when the two portraits were finished, they were hung there, in fine frames, the one next to the other, and everyone said: 'There's a fine couple; they should marry, they would love each other so.' My neighbours, both men and women, laughed when they said this, and did not believe that they were really talking sense; mothers never dreamt in a thousand years of suspecting me, and I believe – may God forgive me – that they would have had no qualms about my sleeping with their daughters; we kissed each other constantly, without incurring their disapproval.

This *vie douce* was marred by jealousy. Mademoiselle ——, who loved me too, soon perceived that I did not love her; I was in no hurry to have her portrait painted. She kept watch on her companion and saw her enter my summerhouse by the little door at the back. She hastened to warn the aunt who at first wanted to upbraid her neice, but the poor child spoke to her so artlessly that she had not the heart to do so.

'My dear Aunt,' she said, embracing her, 'it is quite true that Madame loves me; she has given me a hundred little presents, and she can make my fortune; you know, dear Aunt, that we are not rich. She invites me to come to see her on my own in her summerhouse; I have been there five or six times, but how do you think we pass the time? In clothing Madame, when she is going to make a visit, in dressing her hair, in putting on her ear pendants and patches, in admiring her beauty. I swear to you, dear Aunt, that she thinks only of that; I never cease saying to her, "Madame, how beautiful you are to-day!" and on that she hugs me, and says: "My dear Charlotte, if you could always be dressed *en garçon,* I would love you even more and we would wed; we must find a way of sleeping together without giving offence to God. My family would never agree to it, but we could have a marriage of conscience. If your aunt wishes to come and live with me, I shall give her an apartment in my house, and she will share my table; but I would want you always to be dressed *en garçon;* one of my lackeys would wait on you." And that, dear Aunt, is what we talk about; but, do you not see yourself, if that should happen, should we not be extremely happy?'

These soft words soothed the aunt, and my little love, to play her game the better, took her to the summerhouse.

The first time she came there, I overwhelmed her with compliments, and proposed to her that I should have a simple and quite innocent union with her niece.

She replied that she would agree to whatever I wished.

I then began to prepare everything for the feast of *jeudi gras*.[28] I asked all Charlotte's relations – two first cousins, curriers and tanners, their wives and three of their children; all these came to sup with me. I bedecked myself with all my jewellery and put on a new gown. I had had some new clothes made for the young girl, whom I called Monsieur de Maulny, the name of an estate which brought me an income of two thousand livres, which I wished to give to her.

The ceremony took place before supper, so that the evening would be more festive. Wearing a robe of silver moiré and a small bunch of orange-blossoms behind my head, like a bride, I said in a clear voice, before all the relations, that I took Monsieur de Maulny for my husband, and he said that he took Madame de Sancy for his wife. We touched hands, he put a small silver ring on my finger, and we kissed each other; I forthwith called the curriers and their wives my cousins; they thought that I was doing them a great honour.

After that, we supped uncommonly well, we walked in the garden, and there was singing and dancing. I made little presents to the company, snuff-boxes, embroidered cravats, coifs, gloves, steenkirks. I gave the aunt a fifty-louis ring, and when they were all well disposed in mind, my *valet de chambre*, who had been given the word, came to announce that it was close on midnight. Everyone said that the married couple must be bedded; the bed was prepared and the bedroom well lit; my head was dressed for the night with pretty cornets with many ribbons and I was put to bed.

Monsieur de Maulny, at my request, had had his hair cut like a man's, so that after I was in bed, he appeared in a dressing gown, his nightcap in his hand, and his hair tied up behind with a flame-coloured ribbon. He made a little fuss about going to bed, and then came and lay down beside me.

All the relations came to kiss us, the good aunt drew the bed curtain, and everyone went home. It was then that we gave ourselves to joy, but without overstepping the limits of propriety. That may be difficult to believe but it is none the less true.

The day after our union, or pretended marriage, I had put on my door a notice that the second floor was to let; the aunt took it, and came there to live with Charlotte, who was always dressed as a man in the house, because that pleased me. My valets would not have dared to have called her anything other than Monsieur de Maulny.

Sometimes in the morning I sent for tradesmen to show me materials, so that they would see me in bed with my dear husband; our breakfast was served in their presence, and we would give each other little marks of affection. Afterwards Monsieur put on his dressing-gown and went to dress in his room, while I stayed with the tradesmen to choose my materials. Sometimes there were lively young men who spoke to me of the good looks and charm of Monsieur de Maulny, when he had left the room.

'Am I not happy', I would say to them, 'to have a husband so finely developed and so gentle? He opposes me in nothing; so I love him with all my heart.'

Moreover, we had a well-ordered establishment; for apart from the little weakness I had of passing for a woman, I was without reproach.

I went every day to Mass on foot, to one of the small convents near my house; one lackey carried my train, and the others a black velvet stool for me to kneel on, and my devotional book bag.

Once a week I went, with Monsieur Garnier or the curé, to visit the deserving poor and give them alms; that made me known throughout the parish, and I would hear the women water-carriers and the fruit saleswomen say clearly enough behind my back :

'There is a good lady; God bless her!'

'Why,' said another one day, 'when they are so beautiful, do they love only themselves, and don't love the poor?'

Another time, an apple-seller, when I had bought all her wares to give them to a poor family, said to me, clasping her hands:

'God be with you, my good lady! And may you, by His Grace, enjoy another fifty years as blooming as you are now!'

This naïve praise gave me great pleasure, and I perceived that the curé himself was not unaffected:

'You see, madame,' he said to me, 'that God rewards good works by small human pleasures; you love your face and figure a little too much, you must agree, but because you do good works, you are rewarded for them by the public's acclamation, and we cannot help applauding you ourselves for what we would call weakness in another.'

Such was our discourse on our rounds, and then we would come to the parish church for Mass; my lackeys waited there and I would order them to return at a specified hour to conduct me back to my house.

One day, I risked going to the Comédie with my dear Maulny and her aunt, but I was stared at too much, I was too much the object of attention. Twenty people, out of curiosity, waited at the door for me until we went into our carriage. Some were so impudent as to compliment me on my beauty, to which I made no response, maintaining a modest but haughty countenance; but it was a long time before I returned there; I had to avoid scandal.

The Opéra was not the same; seats there were expensive and, not wanting to miss the performance, the audience was respectfully quiet. I went there at least twenty times without anyone saying anything to me. However, I decided then to stay at home, or at least in my neighbourhood, where I could do as I pleased without being found at fault.

I happened to have a little accident when I was walking in my garden. I gave myself such a severe sprain that I had to keep to my bed for eight to ten days, and to my bedroom for more than three weeks.

I tried to amuse myself; my room was splendid, my bed was

of crimson and white damask, and so were the tapestries, and the window and door curtains. There was a large pier-glass, three big mirrors, a looking-glass over the fireplace, porcelain, Japanese cabinets, some gold-framed pictures, the chimney-piece of white marble, a crystal chandelier, seven or eight *plaques*[29] where, at night, the candles were lit. My bed had a backboard, the curtains were fastened with white taffeta ribbons; my sheets were lace-edged and there were three big pillows and three or four small ones fastened to the corners with flame-coloured ribbons. I was usually sitting up in a Marseilles corset[30] with an *échelle* of black ribbons, a muslin cravat with a large knot of ribbons under the neck, a well-powdered peruke small enough to show my diamond ear pendants, and five or six patches. I was in good spirits, because I was not actually ill at all.

My neighbours, of both sexes, kept me company every afternoon, and I retained five or six of them for supper in the evenings; I sometimes had music, but never any gaming, because I could not abide cards. In this state I received many visits, and everyone complimented me on my attire, which could not be found wanting in modesty, and it may well be remarked that my ribbons were never anything but black.

As soon as my ankle was a little better, I got up and spent my days on a settee, wearing *robes de chambre* which were more seemly than splendid.

However there was no preventing stories being told to the Cardinal that I had robes all of gold, covered with flame-coloured ribbons, with patches and ear pendants of brilliants, and that, so dressed and bedecked, I would go to High Mass in my parish church where everyone who saw me was distracted by my appearance.

His Eminence, who liked everything to be regular, sent an abbé who was one of my friends, in whom he had confidence, to visit me to see how things in fact were. He told me this in all friendship and assured me that he would tell His Eminence that my clothing was seemly and not at all ostentatious, that my robe

44

was black, with tiny golden flowers which could hardly be seen, and lined with black satin, that I had fine earrings of brilliants and three or four small patches, that he found me exactly so when I went to Mass, and that therefore what had been reported was ill-natured scandal.

So I remained untroubled and continued to live a most enjoyable life. That, of course, did not prevent songs [31] being written about me, but I did not object to their being sung.

II

The loves of
M. de Maulny and Mlle Dany

I was greatly enjoying myself, but to tell the truth, we over-stepped ourselves somewhat. We were seen every day at the theatre, the Opéra, at balls, at *promenades publiques*,[32] at Court and even at the Tuileries, and I heard people say, more than once when they saw us pass, 'the wife is a fine woman, but the husband is the more comely.' That did not displease me.

One day I met Monsieur de Caumartin, who is my nephew; he walked with us for some time, but the next day he came to see me and represented to me with some force that I was making too much of an exhibition of myself. He received no response from me other than that I was obliged to him.

The curé, to whom doubtless my relations had talked, spoke to me as well, but he fared no better.

I also received anonymous letters on which I set little store; here is one I kept as an example of how sensitive and intelligent people express their opinions and advice:

I have not had the honour, madame, of making your acquain-tance, but I see you often in church and even in private houses. I know of all the good and charitable work which you do in our parish; I concede that you are beautiful, and I am not

46

surprised that you like women's attire, which greatly becomes you; but I cannot forgive you the *alliance,* I dare to call it scandalous, which you have made openly and before the world with a young girl who is our neighbour and whom you make dress as a man to add a spice to her. It would be one thing if you dissembled your weakness, but you flaunt it; you are seen in your carriage in the *promenades publiques* with your 'husband', and I almost expect that one day you will pretend that you are carrying a child. Think of this, my dear lady, and search your heart. I want to believe that you are guiltless, but one judges by appearances and when one sees your little 'husband' living in your house, and that there is only one bed in your bedroom, where your friends see you daily together, like a husband and wife, is it an unjustified aspersion to assume that you grant each other favours? That you dress as a woman is no cause for gossip, because it harms no one; act the coquette, I will not criticize that, but do not go to bed with someone whom you have in no way married; that flouts all the rules of propriety, and, while it may be no offence in the eyes of God, it is always offensive in the eyes of Mankind. Please, *ma belle dame,* do not attribute this criticism to bad humour, it is simple affection for you; we cannot see you without loving you.

I re-read this letter several times, and I took heed of it; indeed if all the admonitions had been so palatably presented, I would have paid more heed to them than I did. I never went out during the day, and I was more careful than I had been.

I loved her always, and we would not have been parted if it had not been for the chance event which I am going to relate to you.

A very rich bourgeois who knew that Monsieur de Maulny was a girl and that I had never behaved dishonourably towards her, because I thought only of my own beauty, fell in love with her and asked her hand in marriage. He was an Inspector of Timber and owned property worth a hundred thousand francs; he offered to give all this in the marriage contract.

The curé came to tell me about this, her aunt wept and implored me not to stand in the way of her niece's good fortune, and, almost overnight, I watched her turn back into a young and lively woman. She had doubtless told of everything that had passed between us, and had been informed that a genuine husband would give her many more pleasures than I had done, who had merely caressed and kissed her.

I gave my consent to the marriage. I returned all her letters and I gave her many presents, but once the wedding was over I did not see her again; I have never been able to tolerate married women. I was quite wretched, but knew my anguish would not last, for I liked the pleasures of life too much, and Providence soon sent me a new *protégée*.

It was at Madame Durier's, my linen-draper, near the *Doctrine chrétienne*,[33] that I saw a girl who seemed most attractive to me. She was no more than fifteen, she had a fine colour, red lips, good teeth and lively black eyes. I asked my linen-draper how long she had had the girl. She told me only for a fortnight, she was an orphan, she had taken her from charity, and she was the apprentice in the shop.

Four days later, when I was passing by, I called there and was told that my linen was not yet ready. I saw the young girl again and to me she was even prettier than before.

On the following Sunday, I was told at nine o'clock (I had just awakened) that Madame Durier was sending me one of her girls with my linen; I saw her enter and recognized the little girl. Madame had clearly seen that she did not displease me. I made her come to my bedside and told her to show me her wares, which she did very nicely. I then said to her :

'My little darling, come here so that I can kiss you.'

She curtseyed low, came to me and offered her little mouth which I kissed three or four times.

'Would you be pleased,' I asked her, 'if I wished to have you next to me in my little bed?'

'I should be greatly honoured, madame,' she replied; the poor girl believed that I was a woman.

I dismissed her and told her mistress the next day that I wanted to pay for her apprenticeship, and I gave her four hundred francs for that purpose. Little Babet was so full of joy that she could not speak.

'Send her to me this evening,' I told her mistress; 'she will sup with me. I would like to examine her, to see how she is formed, before I do more for her.'

The same evening, I saw the mistress arrive with the girl; the mistress wanted to take her leave, but I kept her back and all three of us supped together. Babet had never eaten partridges, and her mistress only rarely.

After supper, my servants left us, and I said to the linen-draper:

'I am much inclined towards Babet, but before committing myself to her, I would like to see how she is formed.'

I called her to me, I looked at her teeth and her bosom which had begun to form; her arms were a little thin.

'Madame,' said the linen-draper, 'keep Babet tonight; have her sleep next to you. I assure you that she is quite clean; she sleeps with me; you will then be able to examine her body at your leisure.'

That seemed to be a sensible suggestion, so I kept Babet and sent a lackey to fetch cornets for her which were quite plain (she soon had prettier ones).

At my house I had an old maidservant who had been with my mother, to whom I paid a pension of a hundred écus; I summoned her.

'Mademoiselle,' I said to her, 'here is a girl who has been recommended to me as a lady's maid, but I would first like to ensure that she is quite clean in her person. Examine her from head to foot.'

She obeyed me in a trice and made the girl as naked as the back of my hand (there were only the three of us); then she threw a robe over her shoulders. I never saw such a pretty little body; upright, small hips, a burgeoning bosom as white as snow. She then put on her shift, and I said to her:

'My dear, go and lie in my bed.'

I made my toilet, and was soon in bed; I was dying to embrace the little wisp.

'Madame,' said the old servant, 'she will, in two years' time, be the prettiest person in Paris.'

I kissed her three or four times most enjoyably. I put her, all of her, between my legs and greatly fondled her; at first she was too shy to respond to my caresses, but soon lost her reticence and I sometimes had to tell her to leave me in peace.

I sent for Madam Durier and told her that I was taking Babet as my personal maid but, in spite of that, I wished her to learn the linen-draper's trade. She was to work at the shop three times a week, and the other three days she would stay with me, and would be taught how to dress hair. Madame Durier would give her dinner, but every night she would be sent to my house to sleep. This arrangement was faithfully kept.

I obtained neater clothes for Babet and much underlinen. Soon I was quite devoted to her. She went with me everywhere, on visits, to church, and wherever we went she was considered attractive, with a modest and refined air.

My attachment to her increased almost visibly. I could not refrain from dressing her in the most lovely clothes and the finest linen in Paris; I bought for her from Monsieur Lambert, the jeweller, earrings of brilliants, which cost me eight hundred and fifty livres; I had her hair dressed with silver and blue ribbons; I always put seven or eight little patches on her. It was soon evident that she was no longer on the footing of a lady's maid, so I engaged one who looked after her more than me. I asked her what her surname was, and it was quite attractive; I had her called Mademoiselle Dany, and no one referred to her again as Babet.

Who could describe her delight at being made so much of! She owed it all to me, and showed her gratitude continually. I took her to my pew at Saint-Médard and made her sit next to me, to emphasize the favour in which I held her. It went so far that I was more concerned with her fine dressing than with mine, and if it had not been for her I would have neglected my own appearance, but she, in turn, took care of me and thought only of making me wear something which showed me off well.

Mademoiselle Dany restored all my good humour and I began again to entertain my neighbours to supper. One evening I invited the curé, my confessor Monsieur Garnier, Monsieur Renard and his wife, Madame Dupuis and her elder daughter; the younger daughter, who had had an attachment for me, had married a young man who had been given a post near Lille, whither she had gone with him.

When supper was served, we sat down at table, but Monsieur Renard, who had not seen Mademoiselle Dany, asked me where she was. I told him that she would be supping in her room. Everyone begged me to send for her; they knew that this would please me. I gave instructions for her to come down. She soon appeared, as lovely as an angel. Her skirt and mantua were of silver moiré, her head adorned with flame-coloured ribbons, her bosom well exposed. She had no pearl necklace because she had a beautiful neck. I had told her to wear my best earrings and fifteen or sixteen patches. I had rightly suspected that, when she was not seen, she would be asked for.

They all admired her beauty, she sat down at table, and we ate. When the meal was over Mademoiselle Dupuis took from her pocket some large sugared sweets, counted on her fingers that we were eight, and asked me to take eight of them, which I did.

'The most innocent of us, madame,' she said to me, 'must share them out as she pleases.'

The task was given to Mademoiselle Dany who gave us each one haphazardly.

'Oh! break them,' said Mademoiselle Dupuis, 'and you will find inside a little motto.'

This was done. There was: 'I love no one; I love good wine;' *la petite* had: 'To whom shall I give my heart?'

'Oh!' she cried, 'it is all given.'

'And to whom?' she was asked.

She looked at me tenderly, and said nothing.

This was thought most charming: I called her over and kissed her.

'And I, little one, I give you mine.'

Monsieur Renard, who was next to me, made room for her and she remained with me for the rest of the supper. I provoked her a little to make her speak.

'They say that you are pretty, what do you think?'

'My mirror tells me something,' she said, 'But what makes me believe it, is that a beautiful lady has given me her heart.'

'Would you be very upset,' I added, 'if you had smallpox?'

'I should be quite in despair, madame, you would love me no more.'

'And I, my pet, if I had it, would you love me no more?'

'That is not the same,' she replied; 'you have so much *esprit,* my beautiful lady, and so much goodness, that when you are as old as Marguerite (that was my cook), you will still be loved.'

Her lively replies pleased the company, and I kissed her with all my heart; some excellent ratafia was brought and the bottle was soon empty. I had taken some in a small glass, and was sending it back half-full, when *la petite* took the glass from the lackey's hand, and made a little sign asking me for permission to drink.

'Now there is a lovable young person,' said Mademoiselle Renard; 'I am not surprised that Madame loves her so.'

'Alas!' I replied, 'I love her as if she were my younger sister; we share the same bed, we kiss each other and we go to sleep.'

'Oh! madame,' said the curé, 'we do not doubt your good behaviour.'

'I can guarantee that,' said Monsieur Garnier. 'You are right, madame, to love Mademoiselle Dany, but permit me to say to you that she is showing too much bosom.'

'Very well, monsieur,' I said, 'I shall put a steenkirk on her.'

Everyone was against this, saying that it was not the fashion, but I nevertheless told the curé that when I took her to church she would always wear a steenkirk. I kept my word to him, but the steenkirk was so narrow that it concealed nothing, and I often made a pretext of adjusting it so that I could touch her bosom in public.

We left the table and talked of the news. Monsieur Garnier related a fairly amusing local anecdote of a husband who, on returning home from the country in the evening, had found someone in his wife's bed wearing a man's nightcap, and discovered that it was his sister.

Meanwhile Mademoiselle Dany, at my request, had put herself in my bed by the *petite ruelle*,[34] without being seen by anyone. My clock struck midnight and they all rose to go home, but, in passing near my bed, Mademoiselle Renard noticed little Dany there and took a candle to look at her better; she was almost sitting up, wearing a charming cornet with flame-coloured ribbons and a shift embroidered with lace, cut extremely low so that one saw the whole of her bosom, which was by no means pendulous: they were two little apples, quite white, whose shape could be seen, with a little rosebud on each; she had put a large round patch between them to accentuate their whiteness. I had told her to remove neither her earrings nor her patches. It was summer, it was warm, and although she was quite uncovered she had no fear of catching cold. All the company kissed her.

'Let us go home,' said Madame Dupuis, 'and leave Madame to go to bed with that lovely child.'

I called my servants who lit a flambeau and escorted Monsieur Garnier and the curé back to their homes; Monsieur Renard and his wife had merely to cross the narrow street; Madame Dupuis and her daughter, who lived at the Estrapade,[35] waited for my servants to return.

I undressed in front of them, put on my cornets, and went to bed. I first took the child in my arms and kissed her three or four times, not forgetting her bosom; I then put her in the *belle ruelle,* so that Mademoiselle Dupuis could see her more easily. I lifted her shift from behind and clung to her little body, putting my right hand on her breast. As I had taught her, she remained on her back and turned her head to the left, to give me a pretext for moving forward on her, pretending to wish to kiss her.

'See mademoiselle,' I said to Mademoiselle Dupuis, 'see the little ingrate who does not want me to kiss her!'

Meanwhile, I continued to move forward on her; at last, when I was comfortable, she turned her face a little towards me and gave me her little mouth. I kissed her with unbelievable pleasure, without moving my position, wishing to come back to it many times more.

'Do you love me, little heart?' I asked her.

'Alas! yes, madame.'

'Call me "little husband" or "little wife".'

'I prefer "little husband",' she said.

I began to kiss her again, and our mouths could not leave each other, when all at once she cried:

'How happy I am, my darling husband, my little husband of my heart!'

I myself was as happy as she was, but I did not utter a word. At last I lay on my back and we remained for a while, saying nothing and heaving great sighs.

'Admit,' Mademoiselle Dupuis then said to me, 'admit that you really love Mademoiselle Dany.'

'Am I not justified and is she not quite lovable, and am I not well content to be able to love innocently, without offending God or man? You must have heard what Monsieur Garnier said a little while since; I hide nothing from him, and he was willing to vouch for me.'

I was informed that my servants had returned. The ladies went home and we slept together until half past eleven, when we were awoken to go to Mass. It was a feast-day, and we had time only to put on our skirts, a loose robe and coifs.

We were living happily, when a little breeze came from the Cardinal. The Superior of the seminary for old priests, which had just been established in the faubourg Saint-Marceau, had been to tell him that every day I was in my pew, so bedecked, so dressed up, so beautiful, with so many ribbons and diamonds, that he did not venture to take his seminarists there.

It was Mademoiselle Dany who was the cause of this. The good Superior, who had poor sight, mistook her for me, and seeing her in clothes dazzling with gold, had believed in good faith that it was his duty to report this to the Cardinal.

The curé was summoned and questioned, but he replied that nothing new had occurred, that I went to church every day completely without ostentation, and that doubtless Mademoiselle Dany had been taken for me. He nevertheless advised me to go to see the Cardinal, to clothe myself as usual, but to bring also Mademoiselle Dany, dressed to the height.

I went there on a *jour d'audience*. I wore my black gown, a black skirt, with my bodice of silver moiré concealed, a muslin cravat, a peruke with little powder, tiny gold earrings, and velvet *emplâtres* [36] on my temples.

Mademoiselle Dany, by contrast, was well dressed-up, in a costume of gold material adorned with real flowers, her coiffure superb, my earrings of brilliants and seven or eight patches. We waited in an ante-room for the Cardinal to arrive; he was escorting the Duchesse d'Estrées on her departure when he noticed me and came over.

'Monseigneur,' I said, 'I have come to vindicate myself. Please be so kind as to look at my attire; I never dress otherwise when I go to Saint-Médard. If it is not seemly to you I shall change to whatever pleases Your Eminence.'

'You do very well,' he said. 'Now that I have examined you closely I realize that you have been mistaken for the beautiful young lady here.'

55

He asked me who she was, and I told him of her good fortune. He praised my charity, and exhorted me to take care of her.

'Mademoiselle,' he graciously said to her, 'be as good as you are beautiful.'

He then went to grant audience to others; we departed and were well stared at by two hundred monks who were in the ante-rooms. The curé of Saint-Médard was waiting for me in the hall, and I told him of the reception we had had from the Cardinal. He was admitted later, and the next day he told me that the Cardinal had informed him that he had found me quite modestly dressed, and that he was quite content with the situation, but that he had forgotten to thank me for all my charities in the parish.

That, it may be judged, gave me great pleasure. Three months later I went back to an *audience,* at the request of the curé, to make proposals to the Cardinal for a new foundation for twenty orphans in the parish. I offered to rent the necessary house and to give them five hundred livres a year; many rich tanners' wives had agreed to subscribe substantial sums. He listened to me, and promised to go to the premises himself to inspect the project.

I had come on my own this time, without little Dany. The saintly Cardinal was perhaps vexed at this, and told me that I had become a coquette, but that he forgave me because of my good works.

I went fiery red. He had probably noticed that I was showing my bodice of silver moiré, which he had not seen on the other occasion, and that I was wearing the most beautiful ear pendants and seven or eight patches.

'At least,' he said in my ear, 'if you are coquettish, you are also modest. The one compensates the other.'

I curtseyed low and departed. A fortnight later he came to Saint-Médard; the curé had forewarned me so I was in attendance when he alighted from his carriage.

He was determined to go on foot to see the house which I wished to rent for the little orphans and when he had seen it he thought it most suitable. He had walked the length of two streets before he noticed that my robe and my skirts were trailing on the ground, but as soon as he noticed he insisted that my lackeys held my trains, although I had forbidden it from respect for him.

I had not repeated the error into which I had fallen at his last *audience,* and I wore neither patches nor ear pendants.

'Monseigneur,' I rallied, 'you see that I was expecting Your Eminence.'

He burst out laughing, and did not cease to praise my attire.

'One would wish,' he said loudly, 'that all ladies were as modestly dressed.'

There was more than one woman there who thought to herself that I made far more of myself when he was not there.

The orphanage was a success and prospered.

Could it be imagined that anything could mar such a delightful life? It was Monsieur Mansard, the *surintendant des bâtiments,*[37] who, out of friendship, came to warn me that five or six people had asked for my apartment at the Palais du Luxembourg, telling the King that I no longer took any interest in it, that I had a house in the faubourg Saint-Marceau where I stayed all the time, and that although he had taken my part many times he would have to yield in the end, unless I resumed residence at the Palais du Luxembourg.

I believed him, but I regretted it later. I returned to that miserable house and went out in the evening to Monsieur Terrac's, where there was continuous play. I played and played again and lost great sums; I lost all my money and then my ear pendants and my rings; I had nothing left with which to adorn myself.

I was enraged. I sold my house in the faubourg Saint-Marceau, I lost it. I thought no more of dressing myself as a woman and went travelling to hide my wretchedness and shame and to try to dispel my sorrow.

Before I left I placed poor little Dany in a sisterhood where she conducted herself excellently; two years later she became a nun, and I paid her dowry.

III

The Abbé's intrigues with the little actresses
Monfleury and Mondory[38]

I am confident, Madame, that you have enjoyed the story of the Marquise de Banneville. I was delighted to see myself justified to some extent by the example of such a lovable person; however I admit that her example should not set a precedent. The little Marquise could do many things which were forbidden to me, her superb beauty putting her under everyone's protection. But to return to my own particular adventures, we stayed five or six more days in the country, before leaving for Paris and the Palais. The President's[39] wife took the little Montfleury back to her father and made him promise to send his daughter to sup with her sometimes and allow her to stay the night if it became too late. This happened often and the President's wife's carriage would take her home the next day, quite unobtrusively.

Meanwhile the Marquis de Carbon had settled his affairs on his estates, returned to Paris and, as soon as he arrived, came to see me. It was seven o'clock in the evening and in the forecourt he met the President, who was on his way home. They greeted each other warmly, for the President liked the Marquis.

'You have come to see my niece,' he said to the Marquis. 'She is prettier than ever. She is with my wife, and I shall present you to them.'

58

They went in together; the Marquis bowed to *la Présidente* and granted me the honour of the same salutation. A lively conversation began which lasted until the President announced that supper was ready, and begged the Marquis to join us. He allowed himself to be persuaded, but came to regret his decision when he saw the arrival of Mademoiselle de Mondory for whom the President had sent his carriage. The Marquis's jealousy was aroused again. He did what he could to appear in a good humour, but I read his heart and could see that he was under great strain. From time to time he gave me a long, tender, but frustrated glance and sometimes even one of anger. Little Mondory was winning and she overwhelmed me with caresses.

'Let us go, mademoiselle,' she said mischievously, 'it is late. Let us go to our room, we must curl our hair for the morning.'

The Marquis could no longer contain himself; what he had seen had put him in despair. He came and whispered in my ear :

'I leave you to your actress. I shall no longer disturb your pleasures.'

He went abruptly. I had wanted to soothe him with a few little words as I did not wish to lose him, for my heart was keeping its usual course, wavering between her and him.

But I was in truth greatly touched by an incident which occurred on our first visit together to the theatre. We were in a box in the first tier which the President had reserved; his wife, one of her lady friends, the Marquis and I sat in the front. They were playing *Venceslas,* a piece by Rotrou.[40] Little Mondory had the leading part, but when she saw me in the box, beautifully dressed and happy in the Marquis's company, she began to weep so much that her lines could hardly be heard. I began to weep too, realizing that I was the cause of her flood of tears. The Marquis noticed this and said to me, in a low voice :

'Mademoiselle, you still love her.'

'Monsieur,' I replied, 'I shall never go to the theatre again.'

My reply moved him, and without telling me he went to beseech Mademoiselle de Mondory to come to see me; she wanted nothing of this and ran away behind the stage, still crying, and pretending that she had an excruciating toothache.

To remove her wholly from my thoughts I seriously resolved to set out upon some travels, to chase away my sorrows and abandon, if I could, all my childish affectations which were beginning to be unbecoming, and follow something more substantial. I was no longer in the full flush of youth which makes everything forgivable, but I could still pass for a woman if I so desired. I therefore gathered together as much money as I could, put my affairs in the hands of the President, and left for Italy in a *just-au-corps,* carrying a sword.

I stayed there for ten years, in Rome and in Venice, and gave myself over to gaming. One passion drives out another, and that of gaming is the most powerful of all; love and ambitions become less keen as one grows older, gaming remains green and fresh when all else has gone.

Adieu, Madame, I shall relate to you, when you wish, my travels in Italy and England.

1 Philippe, Duc d'Orleans, the brother of Louis XIV. He was commonly known
as 'Monsieur'.

Marie Magd.ne Pioche de Lavergne
Comtesse de la Fayette,
morte a Paris en May 1693

Suite de   Desrochers

Des outrages du temps plus d'un Ecrit vainqueur
Feront vivre son nom au Temple de mémoire ;
De son heureux Génie ils assurent la gloire ,
Lisez chez Sevigné l'Eloge de son cœur .

2 Madame de La Fayette.

IV

The Comtesse des Barres

When my mother died, she enjoyed an income of twenty-five thousand livres: she had had fifty thousand écus as her marriage portion, four thousand francs dowry, which made a capital of eighty thousand francs; a pension of eight thousand francs from a great prince, six thousand francs from a great queen, an old friend; and for all that she left only twelve hundred francs in ready money, jewellery, furniture and a silver service. But she was not a penny in debt.

We were three brothers. I was the youngest; the eldest was *intendant de province,* the next had a regiment, and I myself had ten thousand livres income from inheritances, as much from my father as from an aunt who had made me her heir, and fourteen thousand livres from benefices.

I at once told my brothers that I would like our interests in our mother's estate to be divided up. They had granted me *émancipa-tion* [41] to avoid having to appoint a guardian for me, which would have been inconvenient and with whom one would be forced to discuss all our intimate financial affairs. They agreed to my proposal, surmising that I would treat them handsomely.

For division between ourselves we had nearly seventy thousand francs each of my mother's property. I took, as my portion, the

61

jewellery at twenty thousand francs, furniture at eight thousand francs and the silver service at six thousand francs. That totalled thirty-four thousand francs; there remained due to me thirty-six thousand francs to complete my share. I let my brothers have this, and all that was owing to my mother, her pensions as well as her dowry, which amounted to somewhat more than forty thousand francs. All three of us were content.

I was ecstatic at having the fine jewellery; I had never owned anything except earrings worth two hundred pistoles and a few rings, whereas now I saw myself with ear pendants worth ten thousand francs, a diamond cross of five thousand francs, and three beautiful rings. These were something with which I could dress myself up and appear at my finest, for since childhood I had always liked to clothe myself as a girl; my escapades at Bordeaux are proof of that, and although I was then twenty-two, female attire still became my yet feminine face.

I had no beard at all, as from the age of five or six they had taken care to rub me every day with a particular lotion which killed the hair at its root, provided the treatment was begun early enough. My black hair made my complexion passable, although it was not especially pale.

My eldest brother was always occupied in the *intendance,* the other with the Army, even in winter. Monsieur de Turenne, who had a liking for him, gave him employment throughout the year to ensure his advancement. A winter campaign, when there is no risk of losing one's life, counts more towards promotion than two in summer, when one can be killed at any time. The reason is simple. It is that most young men want to spend the winter in Paris in order to go to the theatre, the Opéra and to entertain women; however there are those who deny themselves this pleasure to advance their careers.

I was now answerable to no one and I yielded to my inclinations. It even happened that Madame de La Fayette, whom I met frequently, seeing me always well-dressed but with ear pendants and patches, told me as a good friend that this was not right for a man, and I would do better by far to dress myself totally as a woman.

On such great authority, I had my hair cut so that it could be better dressed. I had a prodigious amount of it, as was really necessary in those days if you did not want to borrow any. Little curls or ringlets were worn on the forehead, and large ones on each side of the face and all around the head, with a thick roll of hair entwined with ribbons or pearls, if one had any.

I had plenty of women's costumes and choosing the finest, I went to visit Madame de La Fayette, wearing my ear pendants and my diamond cross. She cried out when she saw me:

'Ah, the beauty! So you have followed my advice, and you have done well. We had better ask Monsieur de la Rochefoucauld,' (who was in her room).

They turned me round and round and were quite satisfied.

Women love to have their advice followed, and Madame de La Fayette believed she had a mission to obtain everyone's approval of what she had suggested to me, perhaps a little light-heartedly. That gave me courage, and for two months I dressed as a woman every day. I went everywhere; calling, to church, to a sermon, to the Opéra, to the theatre, and I believed everyone had become accustomed to it; I made my lackeys call me 'Madame de Sancy'.

I had my portrait painted by Ferdinand,[42] the famous Italian painter, who produced a picture of me which people came to see. I was completely happy in my tastes.

I went to the Palais-Royal whenever Monsieur was in Paris. He was almost effusively friendly to me, because we had the same inclinations. He longed to dress as a woman himself, but did not dare, because of his position (princes are prisoners of their rank). In the evenings he would put on cornets, ear pendants and patches, and gaze at his reflection in a mirror.

Fulsomely flattered by his admirers, he gave a great ball every year on Shrove Monday. He ordered me to attend in a loose robe, my face unmasked, and instructed the Chevalier de Fradine to lead me in the *courante*.[43]

It was a splendid assembly; there were at least thirty-four women decked with pearls and diamonds. I was admired, I danced to perfection, and it seemed the ball was made for me.

Monsieur opened it with Mademoiselle de Brancas who was very pretty (she later became the Princesse d'Harcourt), and a moment later he went to dress up as a woman and returned to the ball masked. Everyone recognized him, just as he intended, and the Chevalier de Lorraine tendered him his hand. He danced the minuet and then went to sit amongst all the ladies. He had to be persuaded a little before he would remove his mask, although secretly this was all he wished to do, as he longed to be seen by everyone. It is impossible to describe the extent of his coquetry in admiring himself, putting on patches and then changing their positions. But perhaps I would have been worse. Men, once they think they are beautiful, are far more besotted with their appearance than women are.

Be that as it may, the ball gave me a great reputation and I had quantities of admirers, most of them to amuse themselves, but some quite serious.

It was a delightful life until the odd, or rather, brutal behaviour of Monsieur de Montausier [44] completely upset me.

He had taken the Dauphin to the Opéra in Paris and had left him in a box with the Duchesse d'Usez, his daughter, while he went visiting in the town, as he did not much care for music. The opera had been playing for half an hour when Madame d'Usez noticed me sitting in a box on the other side of the *parterre*,[45] my ear pendants reflecting from one end of the auditorium to the other. Madame was fond of me, she wanted to see me close to and sent La ——, who was attending the Dauphin, to tell me to come over. I went without delay and the young Prince overwhelmed me with compliments; he would have been then about twelve years of age.

I was wearing a white robe with gold flowers and black satin facings, rose-coloured ribbons, diamonds and patches, and was thought to look very fine. Monseigneur wished me to remain in his box, and gave me some of the collation with which he had been served. My heart was full of joy.

Then Kill-joy arrived: Monsieur de Montausier returned from his visiting. Madame d'Usez at once told him my name, and asked if he did not find me wholly to his taste. He considered me for some time, and then said to me:

'I admit, madame, or mademoiselle, I do not know what to call you, I admit that you are beautiful, but have you no shame at wearing such clothing and acting as a woman, seeing that you are fortunate enough not to be one? Go, go and hide yourself; Monsieur the Dauphin finds you very ill as you are.'

'You will excuse me, monsieur,' interrupted the little Prince, 'to me she is as lovely as an angel.'

I was upset and angry. I left the Opéra without returning to my box, determined to abandon all the finery which had incurred such an untoward rebuke. But I found it impossible to make up my mind and I decided to live three or four years in a province where no one would know me, and where I could make myself pretty as I wished until I tired of it.

Having consulted the map, I thought that the town of Bourges would suit me. I had never been there; it was merely a staging post for those en route to the Army, and there I would be able to do as I pleased.

I wanted to reconnoitre the district myself so I left Paris on the Bourges coach with only one *valet de chambre,* Bouju, who had been with me since early childhood. I wore a blond peruke, so that I, who had black hair, would not be recognized on my return there.

We went to the best inn and on the following day walked through the town, which I found agreeable. I learnt that there were no country houses for sale in the neighbourhood, but that the château of Crespon was in the hands of creditors and that it belonged to a Monsieur Gaillot, a *trésorier de France.*

I went to see the house and found the place charming. It comprised a house built in the last twenty years, which was to be sold completely furnished, a park of twenty acres, flower and vegetable gardens, ornamental lakes, a small wood, the whole property being enclosed by a high solid wall. At the end of the park a wide, wrought-iron gate opened on to a stream which might well have taken a boat had there not been several mills, where most of the town's flour was ground. I noticed, however, that opposite the park there was a stretch of half a league where there were no mills, and I could have a little barge there for outings.

I was entranced; I was told that the foreclosure proceedings were being held at the Châtelet in Paris. I had no wish to make a further inspection and left at once for Paris, impatient to have the seigneury of Crespon; the village there was large.

As soon as I arrived to seek out the *procureurs,* whose names and address I had noted, they told me that the estate had been priced at twenty thousand livres, and that to obtain it I had to add a third on to the price, that is to pay twenty-seven thousand livres in all.

I had been assured at Bourges that it was worth more than ten thousand écus; I wanted it, so I 'thirded' (as the phrase was) and left with possession of the estate. It was Monsieur Acarel, my man of affairs, who took it in his name, made a conveyance to me the same day, and left shortly afterwards to go and take possession; I had confided my plan to him.

Monsieur Gaillot received him with delight, for he had made seven thousand francs which he had not expected. Monsieur Acarel told him that the property was for a young widow called the Comtesse des Barres, who wished to come and settle there.

Acarel retained the concierge, and Monsieur Gaillot promised that he would keep an eye on everything until the Comtesse made her arrival.

Monsieur Acarel returned enchanted with my new acquisition and I was burning with impatience to leave, but I was occupied for more than six weeks with my preparations. I wrote to my brothers to say that I was going to travel for two or three years,

66

and that I was granting Monsieur Acarel a full power of attorney.

Bouju had a capable wife who dressed my hair perfectly, but when I told her that I never wished to give up wearing women's clothes, she advised me to continue to have my hair cut in the fashion, which I did. There was then no means of going back.

I had two magnificent costumes made of gold and silver cloth, and four costumes which were simpler but very neat. I had all sorts of adornments, ribbons, coifs, gloves, muffs, fans and so on, rightly judging that I would find none of these things in the provinces.

I dismissed all my valets, by reason of my journey, and paid them; then I rented a small furnished room near the Palais, and Bouju went to rent a house for me in the faubourg Saint-Honoré for a month, where he had my carriage sent with four horses and a saddle-horse. He also engaged a good coachman, a cook, a groom to serve as postillion, a personal maid to dress and powder me and three lackeys, two tall and one short, to carry my train. He had my carriage repainted in ebony, and put on it a badge with a *cordelière* to show widowhood and, when all was ready, he came for me to my little room.

His wife brought me a neat little dress which I put on with coifs and a mask; that was quite correct at that time, and there was no fear of being recognized.

Bouju went to pay the landlady, and we got into a hired carriage, which was waiting for us at the door.

We went to the house in the faubourg Saint-Honoré where my new servants acknowledged Madame, the Comtesse des Barres, as their mistress. They seemed quite content with my appearance, and I promised to treat them well, provided that they served me with devotion and did not quarrel among themselves.

Two days later we left for Bourges. I wanted Monsieur Acarel to settle me in there, so he was in my carriage with Madame Bouju. Her husband and Angélique, my personal maid, went in the stage coach and my cook rode the saddle-horse.

The silver service was in my coach-chests and under my feet was my jewel-box which I never let out of my sight. My furniture, beds, tapestries, clothes and linen were stored in the stagecoach to which my two spare horses were harnessed. It was so heavily laden that, even though it was May and the roads were good, two additional horses were needed.

We left on the same day and kept to the same stages as the public coach, so that I could have my staff to attend to me each night.

At the first overnight halt, when I alighted from my carriage, I saw one of my first cousins at the door of the hostelry, but I did not remove my mask and he realized nothing. The next day we left before he awakened.

When we arrived at Bourges we were to put up at Monsieur Gaillot's. Monsieur Acarel had written to tell him the day and hour of our arrival, and he met us in his carriage a quarter of a league from the town. He came into my carriage and Monsieur Acarel and Madame Bouju transferred to his.

I was well pleased to converse with him privately. He described the whole town of Bourges and seemed to me to be a man of lively intelligence; he had, however, mismanaged his affairs, though what remained left him comfortable enough. We arrived at his house, he presented me to his wife and then led me to his apartment where he left me without further conversation. I formed the opinion that he was not too much of a provincial.

The next day I had my furniture brought to my house, which I found I liked even more than I remembered. However I still had to stay with the Gaillots for four or five days until everything was ready.

I saw no one in Bourges and made no calls. I went only to Mass, and when I observed that people were anxious to see me, I raised my mask for a moment, which increased their curiosity twofold.

Finally I settled in at Crespon. The village curé was an excellent man without being in any way a bigot. He liked good order and gaiety and well knew how to marry the duties of his calling with the pleasures of life. I recognized at once that I would get on with him famously. From the beginning I informed him of my disposition so that he would be accustomed to it. This seemed to me to be only fair and I assured him that I wished him to be unconstrained with me, as I would certainly be unconstrained with him. I told him that I should be a most conscientious parishioner, that I would try to observe Lent as enjoined by the strictest preachers and that I would look after the poor. I begged him to be one of my friends and to come to sup with me as often as he wished, without ceremony. I gave my word that I would not prepare anything specially for him.

For dinner, I always had a good soup and two substantial *entrées,* ample boiled meat and two dishes of *entremets,* good bread and good wine; the roast in the evening was always ready to be put on a spit when someone arrived.

In my village there were two or three families of gentlefolk who were not over-prosperous. The curé brought to visit me the Chevalier d'Hanecourt, who seemed to me to have an unassuming, mediocre mind, but was as handsome as Apollo, and he well knew it. He had been a musketeer and had fought in three or four campaigns, but he found the profession uncouth and after two years he returned to hunt his hares. At first he was most ardent, but his insincere ways left me untouched, and I believed that he found me attractive only because I was rich. I was nevertheless quite civil to him and bore with patience his ceaseless attentions.

When my house was in order I went to Bourges. I chose to wear a simple, seemly costume, with lace of middling quality, coifs which I did not remove when I made my calls, black ribbons and no patches.

I went first to the Gaillots, who took me to the house of Lieutenant-General du Coudray. He was ugly, but had a pleasant face and a lively intelligence. He received me with full ceremony and presented his wife and daughter to me. His wife was fifty, and you could see that she had been a beauty, the daughter was fifteen or sixteen, very dark-complexioned, but so vivacious and good-humoured that she was most likeable.

While I was there the Marquise de la Grise called with her daughter, whom I thought most pretty. I did not have time to scrutinize her properly as it was nearly nightfall, and I returned to my house.

I had formed a friendship with the Lieutenant-General's wife, who returned my call the very next day. I had the pleasure of showing her the rooms, so differently arranged and furnished from those which she had seen before.

My main bedroom was superb; the finest Flanders tapestry, a bed of rose-pink velvet with gold silk fringes, comfortable seats which I had made from my old skirts and a marble chimney-piece. There were as yet no mirrors, but I bought some fine ones a fortnight later.

The Marquise du Tronc had died in her château, three or four leagues from Bourges; her furniture was sold, and I bought at a very good price two pier-glasses, two chimney-glasses, a large mirror and a chandelier.

It can be judged that my room was most attractively appointed. I had, as a set of rooms, an ante-room, a main room, a dressing-room and a gallery turning onto the garden, and at the back of the house, a bedroom, a small private chapel and two dressing-rooms with a private staircase. On the other side of the staircase was a dining-room with a few steps going to the kitchen. I also had lower rooms which I reserved for guests and a corridor which ran the length of the building, where there were five or six rooms with good beds. I do not mention the valets' rooms nor the stables, where nothing was lacking.

I conducted the Lieutenant-General's wife throughout the house and gave her a good dinner, even though she had arrived only at half-past twelve, so that I could not have anything special prepared for her. She begged me to grant her the honour of dining with her the following Thursday and told me that she

70

would ensure the presence of the principal ladies of the town, who were dying to meet me.

I repaired there on the appointed day, having decided that I should wear my best attire; I had so far appeared in Bourges only in informal dress.

I put on a robe backed with silver, embroidered with real flowers and with a long trailing train. My robe was fastened on each side with yellow and silver ribbons and a large bunch at the back to show the waist; my bodice was quite high and padded in front, to make believe that there was a bosom. As a result I really appeared to have as much as a girl of fifteen.

Since infancy I had been made to wear bodices which were tight-fitting enough to cause bulges in my flesh, which had always been soft and plump. I had always taken great care of my neck which I rubbed every night with veal water and sheep's-foot pomade, which makes the skin smooth and white.

My black hair was dressed in large ringlets; I had my big diamond ear pendants, a dozen patches, a necklace of imitation pearls which were lovelier than real ones, and in any case, when I was seen with so much jewellery, no one would have believed that I would have wished to wear anything counterfeit. In Paris I had exchanged my diamond cross, which I did not like, for five ornamental pins which I put in my hair; my coiffure was ornamented with yellow and silver ribbons, but I had no coif. Since it was June a large mask covered my cheeks completely to avoid sunburn. White gloves and a fan completed my outfit. No one could have guessed that I was not a woman.

At half-past eleven I got into my carriage with Madame Bouju to go to Bourges. I arrived at the Lieutenant-General's, where I found his wife about to get into her carriage. When she saw me she wanted to alight and return to her house, but I prevented her when I heard that she was on her way to Mass at the cathedral church; it was the lie-a-beds' Mass, all the belles of the town would be there and all the beaux. I joined her in her carriage and we went together.

I was stared at from right and left; my finery, my dress, my diamonds, the novelty, all attracted attention. After Mass, we passed between two lines of people to go back to our carriage, and I heard many voices in the crowd saying : 'There's a lovely woman,' which I admit gave me pleasure.

The invited company were waiting for us in the house. The Lieutenant-General came to give me his hand when I alighted from the carriage, we went indoors and I found in the apartment the Marquise de la Grise and her daughter, Monsieur and Madame Gaillot and the abbé de Saint-Siphorien, who had an abbey two leagues from Bourges. He was a sprightly old man who retained the gallantry of his younger days.

'Madame,' he said to me, 'I have heard many reports about you, but now I find that you improve upon them.'

I acknowledged his compliments and embraced Madame de la Grise who seemed to me to be a nice, simple woman. She was not more than forty and did not dress herself up; all her pride was in her daughter, who well deserved it.

She was one of those beauties without a fortune, but with small features, a lovely complexion, small ardent eyes, a large mouth, excellent teeth, slightly pouting pink lips, blond hair and an admirable bosom. Although she was sixteen, she appeared to be no more than twelve.

I liked her and made much of her, kissing her five or six times in succession, which delighted her mother. I re-arranged her hair, which was not becoming, and told her in friendliness that she was showing too much bosom, pointing out how to wear her linen collar a little higher. The poor mother could find no words with which to thank me.

'Madame,' I said, 'I have with me a woman who brought me up; she is most skilful; it is she who dresses my hair, and I believe that people like it well enough.'

All the company exclaimed that no one could have better-dressed hair and that one could well see that I came from Paris where the ladies looked so distinguished.

'It is not,' I added, 'that I do not know how to dress my hair on my own, but one is sometimes lazy. However, it is a great advantage for a young lady to be able to do without her maid.'

'Madame,' I said to Madame de la Grise,' if you wish to entrust your daughter to me for a week, I assure you that she will learn to dress her hair perfectly. I shall make her study this delightful art three hours a day. I shall not let her out of my sight, and she will sleep in my bed and be my little sister.'

Madame de la Grise told me that she would like to have the honour of seeing me in my own house to thank me for all the kindnesses I had shown to her daughter. I did not press matters further.

Dinner was announced. We were twelve at table; the fare was sumptuous, but quite badly served. The husband and wife were continually giving contradictory orders so there was shouting without respite. I myself give definite instructions to my staff and then I pay no more attention to them; all goes as best it can, and generally all goes well.

After dinner, we drank a small glass of Turin rosolio;[46] coffee and chocolate were then not known, tea was in its infancy.[47]

At four o'clock we went to a large room where a consort awaited us. It was composed of a theorbo, a treble viol, a bass viol and a violin. A young lady was playing the harpsichord and making a pretence at accompanying them, but although she was doing the best she could, she played very badly. The cathedral organist, who was to have been accompanist, was ill, and the General's wife had insisted on a concert, be it good or bad. It began and at once plunged into cacophony. I could not restrain myself from giving some words of advice to the young lady, that her harpsichord was a tone too low and that in certain passages rests and long pauses must be observed. My advice was some help, but she did not understand enough to profit by it.

'But madame,' said the old abbé de Saint-Siphorien, 'you speak as if you know music perfectly; sit there and be the accompanist.'

The poor girl left her place and everyone was so pressing that I took over.

I first wished to give them some idea of my capabilities, so I played some improvised preludes and the *'Descente de Mars'*, which required great dexterity. The musicians at once realized my calibre and invited me to lead the performance. It gave me little trouble. I accompanied them, reading by sight all kinds of music, even Italian. The concert was played with such accuracy and liveliness that it was eight o'clock before anyone could believe it. Madame Bouju came to warn me that my carriage was waiting.

I did not wish to go out at night wearing my jewellery, so I took my leave of the company and invited them to call on me, which they promised to do.

I had no idea that they would take me at my word so soon. At noon the next day I saw them arrive in a large old coach belonging to the Marquise de la Grise. She and her daughter alighted from it, followed by the Lieutenant-General, his wife and daughter, and the abbé de Saint-Siphorien. He was a good fellow, and everyone enjoyed his company.

I saw their carriage through the window. Although I was veritably in *négligé,* wearing only a dressing-gown of pink taffeta, a tucker, an *échelle* of white ribbons, lace cornets with pink ribbons, no patches and my small gold earrings, I went downstairs and received them as warmly as if I had been finely dressed.

'Mesdames,' I said to them, 'you have now seen me in all my styles.'

'I do not know, madame,' said the old abbé, 'which of all the styles becomes you best, but I have a strong feeling that forty years ago I would have preferred the shepherdess to the princess.'

We laughed. I suggested a stroll in the garden and took them as far as the wood, to give my cook time to set his spit turning. Half an hour later it was announced that the meal was served. The dinner was light but good.

'Mesdames,' I said to them, 'you have had only a simple

74

repast, but there is always as much every day. I do hope that you will come back here often.'

Mademoiselle de la Grise looked prettier than ever to me, and on the pretext of demonstrating to her something on the harpsichord, I talked with her privately.

'My beautiful little one,' I said to her, 'you do not love me.'

By way of response she threw her arms round my neck.

'Speak to me frankly. Would you be happy to spend a week with me?'

She began to cry and embraced me so tenderly that I knew her little heart was moved.

'But,' I said, 'would your dear mother consent?'

'My dear mother is longing for it to happen, but she fears to mention it to you. She is worried that all you said about it was merely by way of a compliment.'

'My dear child,' I said, 'I shall lead the conversation to your coiffure, and we shall see what she says.'

We returned without delay to the others, and, pretending I had some orders to give, I primed Madame Bouju, who, a moment later, walked through the room where we were sitting. I called to her and said:

'Madame, look at the coiffure of Mademoiselle de la Grise; how do you find it?'

She looked her over and said:

'In truth, madame, it is a pity that such a lovely person has her hair so badly arranged for her face.'

She then remarked to us how she had too much hair on her forehead, and that the ringlets for her face obscured it, and concealed her pretty cheeks. I took her up, and said to Madame de la Grise:

'Would you like me to send Madame Bouju to you tomorrow to dress Mademoiselle's hair? You will see what a difference there will be.'

The old abbé interrupted and said to me:

'Is it fair madame, that you deprive yourself of your servants?

Yesterday you offered to Madame de la Grise to take care of her child for a week, and to make her skilled in dressing hair.'

'If the Comtesse', said the General's wife, 'offered as much for my daughter, I should be delighted.'

'Ah, madame!' cried Madame de la Grise, 'You must not trespass!'

'My dear young ladies,' I said to them, laughing, 'I shall take the one who loves me best.'

'It is I! It is I!' they both cried out, throwing themselves round my neck. Their rivalry amused everyone.

'Do not vex yourselves,' I said to them, 'we shall find a means of satisfying both of you one after the other.'

I spoke in this way to encourage the belief that I loved them both equally.

'It is only fair,' said Madame de la Grise, 'that my daughter should be the first, and here she is quite ready.'

'I shall not be jealous,' said the General's wife, 'provided that mine has her turn.'

'As it pleases you', I said to them. 'I am very fond of them both, and I shall be delighted to do them each a little favour.'

It was decided that Mademoiselle de la Grise would stay with me, and that Mademoiselle du Coudray would come afterwards to undergo the same tuition.

The ladies returned to Bourges, and in the evening Mademoiselle de la Grise's caps and linens were brought. I sent for the curé to sup with us. He brought the Chevalier d'Hanecourt with him and I presented my little lodger, smiling with happiness, to them; after supper I dismissed the curé and the Chevalier.

I was impatient to go to bed, and I believed that the girl was as anxious as I was. Madame Bouju dressed her hair for the night and made her go first into my bed, by the *petite ruelle*. I came shortly afterwards and as soon as I was in bed I said to her:

'Come near, my little darling.'

She needed no persuading and we kissed most tenderly; our mouths clung together. I held the little one a long time in my arms and kissed her beautiful bosom. I also made her put her hand on the little that I had, so that she would still be assured that I was a woman. But I went no further the first day, contenting myself with the knowledge that she loved me with all her heart.

The next day we made several calls in the neighbourhood; the *petite* became bored and whispered to me:

'*Belle dame* (that was the name she decided to give me) I find the day very long.'

I understood what she meant. As soon as we were in bed there was no need to tell her to come near, she wanted to devour me with caresses. I was bursting with desire and I set myself to give her real pleasure. She began to say that I was hurting her, then she gave such a cry that it raised Madame Bouju from her bed to see what was happening. She found us as close as we could be; the *petite* was weeping, but nevertheless had the spirit to say to Bouju:

'Madame, it is a cramp to which I am subject which gave me such great pain.'

I kissed her fervently, and did not relinquish my hold.

'Oh, that hurts!' she cried again.

'Mademoiselle,' said Bouju, who was a cunning old woman, 'that will pass and, when you feel no more pain, you will be pleased and comfortable.'

Indeed the pain soon vanished, the tears of suffering became tears of pleasure. She held me with all her strength and said not a word.

'Do you love me, my darling?' I asked her.

'Alas yes! I am beside myself, I do not know what I am doing. You will always love me, *belle dame,* won't you?'

I made my reply with five or six wet kisses and began my performance again. This time was less painful than the first and the *petite* did not cry out, but only sighed deeply.

We did not allow our pleasures to distract us from our promise to her mother. Bouju began instructing her to dress her hair, but

77

I told her to spin out the lessons to last at least a fortnight. I was beginning to dread the departure of my little love and thought of her successor only with disdain.

Three days later Madame de la Grise came to dine with us. I had told the little one that she must not divulge how much we loved each other; she made this reply to me:

'Oh, I shall take good care, *belle dame*, not to tell my mother of the delights we have together. She would be so jealous, for she and I almost always share the same bed, but we are never so happy. But I do love my dear mother, though I love *belle dame* more, a thousand times more.'

The poor child's innocence pleased me and also saddened me a little, but I dismissed any thought that might have spoiled my happiness.

Madame de la Grise thought her daughter's hair very well dressed, but wished she had had the pleasure of seeing her dress it herself.

'Madame,' I said to her, 'spend the rest of the day with us and you will see tomorrow how she sets it herself. I have a large bed which you and I can share, and the girl will sleep with Bouju.'

After a little persuasion she agreed. I immediately regretted my offer as it would be a night wasted. But, on the other hand, it would be a marvellous way of ensuring the mother's confidence. We dined, we took a turn in the park, and in the evening I made Mademoiselle de la Grise recite some verse.

I was a good actress, it was my first occupation.

'I have chosen,' I said to the mother, 'a moral, Christian play (it was *Polyeucte*);[48] she will find there nothing but noble sentiments.'

The girl spoke the verses badly enough, but I sensed that with a little application she would speak them as well as I; she understood them, and understanding is half the art of declaiming.

Madame de la Grise could not cease thanking me. I confidentially made some small criticisms of her daughter: that she did not hold herself upright, that she was slovenly, that she did not put away the clothes that she had worn, so that she scolded her a little. This did wonders, and convinced her that I was interested only in her daughter's welfare and that I was not infatuated with her.

We supped and went to bed; clean sheets had been put on for Madame de la Grise. When we were in bed, I approached her and kissed her two or three times, and then returned to my side, saying:

'Let us sleep, madame. That is how I treat your child, and I assure you she sleeps like a log. She works and takes exercise all day, she even runs in the garden with Angélique, so she needs her sleep.'

The next day, the poor mother was in ecstacies when she saw her daughter twist a ringlet with surprising adroitness. Bouju said to her:

'I assure you madame, that in a fortnight Mademoiselle will know as much as I.'

We dined, and Madame de la Grise departed, which gave us much pleasure.

'How we shall kiss tonight!' said the little one. 'It seems ten years since I embraced *belle madame*.'

As soon as we had supped we went to bed; we had to make up for lost time. There was nothing out of the ordinary in our love-making, the poor child knew no subtleties.

Four or five days later, the Lieutenant-General's wife, her daughter, Madame de la Grise and the good abbé came to dine and pass the day with us. The du Coudray daughter, who was a lively girl, kept on saying:

'Really, Mademoiselle de la Grise is a long time in learning to dress hair. I believe that I could have mastered it in four lessons. A week was asked for, and now more than two have gone by.'

She believed that she was advancing her suit, but she retarded it for I wished she were far away. I adored my little love and, as for her, I did not like her at all.

We had three weeks of pleasure. Mademoiselle de la Grise

79

dressed her hair quite perfectly so I took her back to her mother, but I insisted that on that day she did her hair quite unaided, without Bouju putting a finger on it. Before we left I put on her ears two small earrings of a single ruby surrounded by tiny diamonds, very pretty.

'I would like to give you a more handsome present,' I told her, 'but, dear heart, people would talk.'

Madame de la Grise was delighted. She showed her to everyone, affirming that I had given my word that she had dressed her hair unaided. She made a little fuss about allowing her to accept the earrings.

'It is nothing.' I told her. 'I have had them since I was a girl, they do not become me.'

The Lieutenant-General's wife said, laughing:

'If the Comtesse gives as much to my daughter, I shall be quite happy.'

That was to offer her to me and I had to take her, as I had promised. I took her to my home and kept her for only a week. Bouju taught her hair-dressing so quickly that even I was astonished.

She was a lively, spirited, eager girl, who dressed her hair in the morning and, instead of taking a walk, undid it in the afternoon so that she could dress it again in the evening. She slept in my bed. I kissed her when we were in bed and she gave me little caresses, but I risked nothing with her. Apart from being less lovable than Mademoiselle de la Grise, I thought her quicker and perhaps more knowing. She would never have believed, like Agnès, that babies came through the ear. She was an accomplished flatterer, and perhaps I would have loved her had I not met the other girl first.

At last, at the end of the week, I brought her in triumph back to Bourges. She really understood how to dress hair and believed that she had gained a victory by having learnt it in so short a time. Her mother shared in her triumph.

80

Mademoiselle de la Grise admitted that it had taken her a month to learn as much :

'You understand how it is, *belle dame,*' she said to me privately. 'I care little that everyone thinks that I am stupid and slow, as long as you think otherwise.'

Two days later the news came that the *intendant* had arrived at Bourges to assess taxes. He was called Monsieur de la Barre and had previously been *intendant* at Auvergne. He later became a soldier, did some brave deeds in the war, and became Viceroy of Canada, where he died.

I thought that it was my duty and in my interest to go to see him. I went quite simply dressed, wearing only my diamond ear-rings and three or four patches.

The Lieutenant-General's wife presented me and I was received most warmly. It appeared that he had already heard of me.

Three or four days later the Lieutenant-General's wife advised me in the morning that he would be coming to see me the next day, and that he had invited her to be one of the party.

I prepared a little reception for him. I put on the best dress that I had, I dressed my hair with yellow and silver ribbons, my big ear pendants, a pearl necklace, a dozen patches; nothing was overlooked in my adornment.

He arrived at noon with the Lieutenant-General, his wife and daughter. As soon as I saw his carriage in the drive I went downstairs to receive him. *Intendants* are kings in the provinces, one cannot do them too much honour.

He seemed impressed with the beauty of my house and the elegance of my furniture. I suggested a stroll in the garden while we waited for dinner. The curé and the Chevalier d'Hanecourt helped me to do the honours.

Half an hour later we returned to the house and Madame and Mademoiselle de la Grise arrived with the abbé de Saint-Siphorien. We sat down at table, the fare was both sumptuous and delicious. All was well.

After dinner we went through to my reading-room, where an

ensemble was waiting. I had brought the musicians from Bourges and I sat at the harpsichord to accompany them.

'But,' said the *intendant*, 'is the Comtesse a musician as well?' I made reply with three or four pieces by Chambonnière,[49] which I played solo, and then the recital began.

The consort consisted of a treble and a bass viol, a theorbo, a violin and my harpsichord; we played only pieces which we had rehearsed thoroughly. The *intendant* seemed charmed.

We played until six o'clock in the evening when a walk was proposed. Earlier we had been only as far as the entrance to the park, but this time we went up to the iron gates and saw on the river a barge which I had prepared a short while before. There were well-padded seats and in the middle was a long table covered with all the fruits of the season. The young ladies were delighted and could not wait to feast themselves on the peaches.

We remained on the river for more than an hour and a half and when we had finished our collation I proposed some acting to amuse the *intendant*. I had taught Mademoiselle de la Grise a scene from *Polyeucte*.

'Come, mademoiselle,' I said to her, 'take monsieur *l'intendant's* hat, it will bring you luck. You will be Sévère and I Pauline.'

We began, but the astonished *intendant* could not stop making exclamations.

'I have heard la Duparc,' he said, 'but her performance does not approach that of the Comtesse.'

'Eh! monsieur *l'intendant*,' I said to him, 'it is my first occupation. I had a mother who formed a company from her neighbours, and every day we played *Cinna* or *Polyeucte* or some other play by Corneille.'

La Grise's daughter did not act badly, but it was growing late so we went back into the park. By now the carriages were waiting and the company went home quite content with the entertainment I had provided. My parish also did quite well out of it as the curé had not forgotten to plead its cause to the *intendant*.

Madame de la Grise had need of the *intendant* as much as I, and also wished to fête him; she asked my advice when I went to see her one day at Bourges. I counselled her to give a good supper and a ball, but no concert, because we could not give him anything new in that respect. She told me she would need a week for preparation, and she begged me to come to her house to supervise her arrangements.

'And I shall, if you wish it, madame,' I added laughingly, 'even make myself an actress again for your sake; Mademoiselle de la Grise acts her part quite adequately.'

'But, madame, my daughter acts so badly beside you.'

'It is surprising,' I said, 'that she acts so well. I had given her only five or six lessons; if she had as many again, she would surpass me. Indeed a little journey to Crespon would not be without its uses, she would also improve her skill at dressing hair.'

'Madame,' said Madame de la Grise, 'you have given so many kindnesses to my daughter, I fear to take advantage of you.'

She did not hesitate to summon her.

'Daughter,' she said, 'would you like to spend five or six days with the Comtesse?'

She did not reply but ran straight to her room to pack her little bundle, returning with it under her arm.

'It appears, my dear daughter, that you are hardly distressed at leaving me?'

'Dearest Mother,' she replied, 'I am always delighted to go with the Comtesse.'

Her reply was so tactful and understanding that we both embraced her.

I went back to my house. There was great delight in the house when they saw the young girl; they loved her, and all the servants had seen that I loved her devotedly.

'Mademoiselle,' said Bouju to her, 'have you come again to learn something? You are accomplished at curling, but you do not know how to do the tapé so well.'

We supped; it was late and we were longing to go to bed. The night was more delightful than it had ever been; a short absence whets the appetite.

The next day I had a feeling that I had been neglectful, and that, for more than six weeks, I had given no sign of life to the Gaillots. I at once sent my carriage to them with a letter in which I implored them to spend two or three days in their house, of which they were still the owners.

They needed no pressing and arrived before midday. They wanted to sleep in the dormitory as they knew the beds there and could select the best.

I entertained them as best I could. We went for a walk after dinner; they wanted to see every inch of the park, and praised all the improvements I had made. Eventually their cries of wonder were making me and Mademoiselle de la Grise yawn; they realised this a little tardily and apologised profusely.

'It will be nothing', I told them, 'once we have had a good sleep.'

After we had supped Madame Gaillot begged me to go to bed.

'I am not accustomed to going to sleep so early,' I said, 'but I would not mind going to bed; that will rest me, provided we continue to talk until midnight.'

Bouju came, and also Angélique, my other personal maid. I was curled, my hair put in curl-papers, and they affixed my night bonnet. I put on a dressing-jacket embroidered with Alençon lace, and replaced my diamond earrings with little gold ones. My patches fell off of their own accord and I went to bed between two sheets.

'There is no other woman like you,' said Madame Gaillot, 'and one has to be as beautiful as you are to have so little need of artificial improvements; your mirror is enough and tells you all the time that you have everything yourself.'

Mademoiselle de la Grise was there, standing bolt upright.

'Come along, little girl,' I said to her, 'come to bed, you are as tired as I am.'

Angélique undressed her in a moment and she put herself in

the *petite ruelle*. Monsieur and Madame were in the *grande ruelle* and had begun to tell me a story which had just reached Bourges, when I said to Mademoiselle de la Grise, who was looking solemn :

'Come here, my child, come and say good-night. Then you can go to sleep, we do not want to oblige you to listen.'

She came over and I took her in my arms and made her pass over to the *grande ruelle*. She was on her back and I was on the left side, my right hand on her breast, our legs intertwined. I bent completely over her to kiss her.

'See,' I said to Madame Gaillot, 'she is quite unfeeling. She makes me do the running and does not respond to the affection I give her.'

Meanwhile I was advancing the engagement, kissing her mouth which was redder than coral, and giving her at the same time more solid delights. She had not the control to restrain herself and said, half aloud, with a great sigh :

'Ah! That's wonderful!'

'Have you woken so soon, *ma belle demoiselle*?' asked Monsieur Gaillot.

She realized that she had made a gaffe.

'That is true,' she said. 'I was starved with cold when I got into bed, and now I am so warm and so comfortable.'

I stopped kissing her and lay on my back as well.

'She does not like me,' I told them, 'and you see I like her well enough.'

'But', said Madame Gaillot, 'how could she not love such a lovely lady?'

'It is not true,' said the girl, sitting up, 'I love the lady with all my heart.'

At the same time she threw herself on me unrestrainedly and kissed me with such feeling that it showed that all was well.

'Each one in her turn,' I said to her. 'You were as cold as ice a moment ago, now I would like to be so, but I have not the strength.'

Saying that, I put her back in her place and, under cover of kissing her, took once more the position fitting for our real pleasures. The spectators increased the delight even more; it is sweet to deceive the eyes of the public.

Afterwards we lay back quietly on the bolster; our heads were close to each other and our bodies were even more closely joined.

'*Mon fils*,' said Madame Gaillot to her husband, did you ever see two more charming countenances?'

'It is true', I said, 'that my little love is very pretty.'

'And you, *belle dame*, you are not pretty, you are as beautiful as an angel.'

And saying that, we kissed each other.

'My child is very pretty,' I said to Madame Gaillot, 'but I myself am old beside her; you must not forget that I am twenty.'

That is how the evening passed. Our guests went away and we fell asleep.

The next day the curé and the Chevalier d'Hanecourt supped with us. Madame Gaillot urged me to go to bed and hold a *ruelle* as I had done the evening before.

'It is not the same thing,' I replied. 'There are more people here and it requires more notice.'

Nevertheless I allowed myself to be persuaded.

'You should not feel constrained on my account,' said the curé.

The girl went to bed too and came quite close to me; our heads were touching but we did not kiss.

'Don't you love each other today?' asked Madame Gaillot. 'You do not kiss each other.'

'But', I laughed, 'perhaps the curé would not approve.'

'I, madame? What could be more innocent than an elder kissing a younger sister?'

With that permission I made Mademoiselle de la Grise move, just as the night before, to the *grande ruelle* next to our guests. She lay on her back, for she knew well enough how to place herself by now, and I moved over her to kiss her.

It was a long kiss, and we had never had so much pleasure

before. I left her mouth from time to time to lean my head on the bolster next to hers, but without changing the position of our bodies.

'She is my little wife,' said I to the curé.

'Then you are my little husband!' cried *la petite*, opening her eyes.

'I accept that,' I said to her. 'I shall be your little husband and you will be my little wife, and there is the curé who will give his consent too.'

'With all my heart,' he laughed.

'And I,' said Monsieur Gaillot, 'I offer to suckle all the children which come from the marriage.'

While they were enjoying themselves we were enjoying ourselves too. I had taken my little wife to me again and I kissed her better than I had ever done; we did not utter a word, except at times, 'My little husband, my dear heart!' and many sighs.

'That is settled,' said Madame Gaillot, 'the Comtesse is married, her suitors will have to seek their fortunes elsewhere.'

She said that with some malice on account of the Chevalier d'Hanecourt, who had been unable to speak for laughing at what we were doing.

We sat ourselves up again and spread little furred capes over our shoulders as it was beginning to get cold. Then we conversed quite animatedly. I read my letters from Paris (they are avid for news in the provinces), and they finally went to bed.

The following days passed just as agreeably; our marriage became a standing joke; the Gaillots returned to Bourges and told everyone, and when Madame de la Grise came to see me, she said, laughingly :

'What, my fine fellow! You have married my daughter without telling me?'

'At least, madame,' I said, 'it took place in good company and in the presence of the curé.'

'Madame,' she said, 'my house is now prepared, will you please come to see it? It is Thursday today, and it is on Sunday that I am giving supper to the *intendant*.'

I promised that I would be at her house the next day at three o'clock in the afternoon. I kept my appointment, but I did not bring Mademoiselle de la Grise with me. I told her mother that she had a migraine, that I had made her go to bed, and that we would both come to dine with her on the Sunday.

'We shall have plenty of time to dress,' I said. 'The *intendant* will not arrive at your house until eight o'clock in the evening.'

I thought that the house had been well arranged; a big room for the valets, Madame de la Grise's bedroom for the ball (her bed had been removed), her private room, which was big enough, as a retiring room which would greatly ease the press in the ball-room, and her temporary bedroom as a dressing-room.

I approved of everything and returned thence to Crespon; there I found my little wife, who was as happy as I.

We had still three days together and they were well employed. The curé kept us company in the evenings; the Chevalier d'Hanecourt did not come as he was ill or pretended to be so; he was somewhat jealous.

On the Sunday, having attended High Mass, I got into my carriage with Mademoiselle de la Grise and Bouju. We brought all that we needed to dress for the evening. Our hair had been curled the night before and put in curl-papers.

We had a light dinner because we wanted to begin to prepare ourselves for the evening. I insisted that Bouju first dressed Mademoiselle de la Grise's hair, for she was to be Queen of the Ball.

When she was finally robed and her hair dressed, I removed the ruby earrings which I had given her, and replaced them with my lovely diamond ear pendants. Her mother protested that she would not allow it, but I told her with such earnestness that she was hurting my feelings that in the end she gave her consent. I also put my diamond hair pins in her hair. I was enraptured to see her looking so beautiful, and I kissed her from time to time for my pains.

'But you, madame,' said Mademoiselle de la Grise, 'you will have nothing for yourself, though it is true that you are so beautiful that you do not need adornment.'

I also put a dozen patches on my little wife; provided they were small, one could not put on too many.

As for myself, I wore a splendid gown, my hair was well arranged, I had a pearl necklace and ruby ear pendants, which were not real, but people believed that they were fine stones. How could anyone think that the Comtesse, who had so much beautiful jewellery, would wear anything imitation?

There were twelve ladies invited to supper and each one had to have an escort to take her to the first *courante*.

At seven o'clock everyone had arrived except the *intendant*, who did not come till eight. We stayed in the *cabinet* until supper, and carrying out what we had planned, we recited two scenes from *Cinna*. The girl spoke marvellously, and it was the general opinion that I was a good instructress, but also that she was a good pupil.

Two tables had been laid in the ballroom, each with twelve covers, served without precedence; the ladies divided themselves between them. The supper was excellent.

At half-past ten, the company returned to the *cabinet* and the ballroom was prepared. The candles were lit and the ball began at eleven o'clock, beginning with the *courante* and after that the lesser dances.

At midnight Madame de la Grise was informed that there were maskers downstairs who asked to be admitted; we were delighted. Two groups of them appeared, quite presentable, and were made to dance as soon as they arrived, but there was one masker who was pre-eminent; his clothes were magnificent and he danced perfectly, but no one recognized him. I danced often with him and was dying to know who he was but he refused to remove his mask. I took him to the *cabinet* and I was so insistent when we were alone that he showed me his face. He was the Chevalier d'Hanecourt.

I confess that I was moved by his gallantry, and I asked him not to remove his mask. Since he had come to the ball only on my account, his identity would never have been guessed. He had spent a year's income on his clothes. He slipped out without being noticed and returned home.

We danced until four o'clock, and Madame de la Grise would not hear of my going home at that hour; she had had clean sheets put on the bed in her small room and I slept there. She insisted on sharing her maid's bed with her daughter.

I returned to Crespon the next day and supped with the curé and the Chevalier d'Hanecourt. I treated the latter more kindly than usual and paid him several compliments, which emboldened him to disclose to the curé his intention of offering me his favours. He saw me as a rich attractive young widow, and he wanted to marry me.

The curé, acting as his friend, put the proposal to me, but somewhat distantly. I rejected it even more so.

'Monsieur,' I said to him, 'I am a happy woman and my own mistress, I do not wish to put myself into slavery. I admit that the Chevalier is a pleasant man and I shall try to find some opportunity of pleasing him, but I will not marry him.'

After that, I told him that I was disturbed that the Chevalier had had such fine clothes made simply for love of me. I gave him a purse in which there were a hundred louis d'or and requested him to put it on the Chevalier's table without his noticing, and that if he ever mentioned it to me, I would deny all knowledge of it. The curé praised my generosity and said that I could have found no better use for it.

There were no more than three weeks left of the *Carnaval*[50] when a company of actors arrived at Bourges; I was soon informed of this by the Lieutenant-General's wife who invited me to supper after the performance. I went to see it and I enjoyed it.

Monsieur du Rosan, who took the lover's part, acted as well as Floridor,[51] and there was a young girl of fifteen or sixteen who, although she acted only maid's parts, I singled out as being a very good actress. The rest of the performances were mediocre.

In provincial towns performances are given every evening,[52] and to save me the trouble of travelling back to Crespon each night, Madame de la Grise proposed that I should spend the *Carnaval* at her house.

'Madame,' she said, 'you will not inconvenience me in the least. I shall sleep in my little room and I shall give you the main bedroom with a dressing-room for your maidservants.'

'But', I replied, 'where will Mademoiselle de la Grise sleep?'

'The Beauty', she replied, laughing, 'insists that she be with her husband.'

'I agree to that,' I replied, joining in her laughter.

In this way, throughout the *Carnaval*, I did what I wanted without the girl suspecting anything amiss. She was still innocent but it was no longer as it had been with the *petite* Montfleury.

The next day I went to my house and gave orders that every day I should have delivered at Bourges fat capons which had been raised in my poultry-yard, vegetables from the kitchen-garden and winter fruits, of which I had a good store. They were most gratefully received in Madame de la Grise's kitchen.

We went to the theatre every day. After two or three days I sent for du Rosan and told him that the little actress was capable of playing much more important parts.

'That is true, madame,' he replied, 'but our leading actresses will never consent to such a thing, unless perhaps you could use your influence.'

I spoke to the *intendant,* who was so courteously reasonable and persuasive that the following day Mademoiselle Roselie (that was her name) took the part of Chimène in the *Cid*; she acquitted herself well.

I was taken with the girl, she was extremely pretty, and I was born to love actresses. I made her come to my house, where I gave her some good advice.

'*Ma belle*,' I said, 'there are some passages when the verse must be said quite rapidly and others quite softly; the tone must vary : sometimes high, sometimes low. You must fix in your head that you are Chimène, forget the audience and weep when it is time to do so or at least make a good pretence.'

I demonstrated the lesson which I gave to her. She soon realized that I was a past mistress. The very next day she played in the way I had taught her and her aunt and all the actors thanked me.

'She is a treasure', I told them, 'that you possess without knowing it. She may well become the best actress of her time.'

The applause of the public confirmed this view and their share of the takings, which daily increased, was an even better persuasion. The young girl was enchanted at finding herself treated royally and fêted by everyone.

During this time the Archbishop of Bourges arrived. He was a good man, no wonder-worker, but correct in his conduct, although he liked harmless pleasures. The Lieutenant-General's wife brought me to his house where he received me most cordially and spoke about my house, of which he had been painted a rather flattering picture. He promised to come to see it and I begged him to do me that honour.

On the Sunday before Shrove Tuesday I went to Crespon to prepare everything for his reception. My rooms were well enough appointed, but I had an improvised stage, which needed a hundred candles to illuminate it, erected in one room. I wished to put on a play for the good Archbishop without his knowing anything about it. The actors were instructed secretly.

He arrived at four o'clock on the Sunday afternoon. As the sun was shining I took everyone for a walk in the flower garden, but the cold soon chased us indoors. It seemed that all the ladies of Bourges had come. I took the Archbishop to the 'theatre' and sat him down in an armchair, not without protest from him.

3 A lady wearing a steenkirk and patches.

4 A lady *en deshabillé negligé.*

'You are in the country, monseigneur,' we said to him, 'so this does not signify.'

The play began before he had a chance to back out, but as it was *Polyeucte*, a religious work, he was content.

Roselie played Pauline and entranced the whole company. The good Archbishop summoned her, he longed to kiss her but dared not. I kissed her for him and began to fall seriously in love with her and to regard her as my own product.

Supper followed the play; it was good and we sat for a long time. The Archbishop's health was drunk and it was midnight before everyone returned to the town, except Madame de la Grise and her daughter who were staying with me. I had asked her, and I had my motives for doing so, to lend her carriage to take back the actors after they had eaten a good supper, as mine did not suffice. I gave her in turn the bed in my main bedroom, but this time I was tricked because she made her daughter sleep with her.

The next day I returned to Bourges with them, under the pretext of going to thank the Archbishop, but really to see Roselie whom I greatly desired to have on her own for three or four days at Crespon.

I went to the theatre two hours before the performance began. All the actors and actresses came to thank me; they were delighted with Roselie. I took her aunt on one side and told her that she must not wear out her niece by making her play every day, as she was taking leading parts which often entailed her having to deliver five or six hundred verses. Instead I suggested she should appear only twice a week.

'I see that well, madame,' said the good aunt, 'but our colleagues think only of making money and when Roselie appears the audience is very much bigger.'

'Give her to me,' I said. 'Today is Monday, I shall bring her back to you on Thursday and in future, believe me, make her play only on Sundays and Thursdays, that will give her a rest.

I promise you that I shall make her rehearse her part. She will have no more difficulty with it.'

She thanked me warmly and I brought her niece to stay with me at Crespon.

It can easily be guessed that she slept with me. I caressed her with my utmost address and I wanted to put her from the first on the same footing as Mademoiselle de la Grise, but she resisted.

She was really a good girl, I realized that afterwards, but she was more worldly than the little la Grise; an actress of sixteen knows more than a young lady of quality who is twenty. I urged her. She was beholden to me and could clearly see that I loved her. I promised never to leave her. I held her in my arms and kissed her passionately, our mouths could not leave each other, our two bodies became one.

'Trust me,' I said; 'you see, dear heart, that I trust you. My secret, without which there can be no peace in my life, is in your hands.'

She made no reply but sighed. I pressed her more and more until I felt that her resistance was weakening, then I redoubled my efforts and finished with that kind of contest in which the winner and the loser dispute who has had the triumph.

It seemed to me that I had even more pleasure with her than with Mademoiselle de la Grise; the rank and innocence of the one were well replaced by the pretty ways of the other, who had all the charms of coquetry.

This first venture grew into our way of life. Her pleasure easily persuaded her that I would love her always and she overwhelmed me with affection. I was forced to adjure her to restrain her loving behaviour when we were in the public eye, although we knew how to give each other the strongest marks of affection without fear of scandal.

I did not fail to take Roselie back to Bourges the following Thursday; they found that her performance grew continually better and better.

I went to sup at the Lieutenant-General's; Mademoiselle de la

Grise was there, almost slovenly in her dress and quite wretched. I still loved her, though the little actress had taken first place, and I asked her in a most friendly manner what was wrong with her. Immediately she burst into tears, and fled. I spoke to her again after supper.

'Alas, madame,' she said, 'how can you ask what is wrong with me? You do not love me any more, and you are going to sleep with Roselie at Crespon. She is more attractive than I, but she does not love you so much.'

I let her speak and was wondering how to reply, when her mother requested me to go to her private room where she told me that the Comte des Goutes had asked for her daughter's hand in marriage.

He was a man of noble birth and of the locality, who had an income of eight to ten thousand livres. I advised her not to miss the opportunity, as much to free myself from the importunity of the girl as because she was a good little thing, and also because of remorse. I had always feared that our relationship might produce an undesirable and indeed, bizarre result which would have thrown everyone into confused discomposure, whereas with Roselie I went free and at full tilt, without fear of committing indiscretion.

A week later the betrothal of Mademoiselle de la Grise and the Comte des Goutes was announced. I went to Bourges to give them my best wishes.

I felt myself obliged, in honour and in conscience, to give some advice to Mademoiselle de la Grise.

'My dear child,' I said to her, 'you are going to be married, so you must try to be happy. Your husband is personable, he seems a thorough gentleman, he loves you, but he will not always be so loving and you must be prepared to forgive his moods. You are a good and sensible person, and must never give him cause for jealousy. Think only of pleasing him, devote yourself to your household and cherish your children, if God's grace grants you

95

them; they are the blessings of a marriage and the sweetest bond between married people.'

'But listen to me, dear child; I think that you will remember those blissful nights we spent together. Be sure to remember, on your wedding night, to behave with your husband as you did with me, but with him it must be deliberate, whereas with me it was instinctive. Let yourself be urged and pressed for some time, struggle, weep, cry, so that he believes he is teaching you what I have already taught you; on that depends your life's happiness. I am opening your eyes now because it is absolutely necessary; you must not worry about our secret; I am just as interested as you in seeing it kept.'

The poor child burst into tears. Her mother came into the *cabinet.*

'Madame,' I said to her, 'she is crying. We must admire her modesty.'

Her mother kissed her.

'My daughter,' she said, 'you owe much to the Comtesse; follow her advice which she gives and hide your tears.'

We went back into the room to rejoin the company. The next day the Archbishop himself married them, and three days afterwards the married couple went to their estate which was seven leagues from Bourges. I promised to go to see them, and I kept my word two months later.

She was already pregnant and I found she was quite taken with her husband and the pleasure of having a well-run house. It was indeed a pleasure for a young woman, straight from under her mother's wing, to be mistress of her own house. It seemed to me that she was still by no means indifferent to me, but in the end her virtue did for her what my fickleness had done for me.

After Easter the Archbishop returned to Paris, the *intendant* was no longer at Bourges, and all the nobility who had spent their winter there had returned to their respective villages. The actors were not taking enough to pay for their candles and they too announced their departure.

96

Roselie cried night and day in fear of leaving me; I was as upset as she. I brought her aunt to Crespon and told her I wanted to make her niece's fortune, and that if she wished to hand her over to me, I would take her to Paris in six months' time and have her admitted to the Hôtel de Bourgogne.[53] Her talent and my friends made me confident of succeeding in this plan. I gave weight to my proposal with a purse of a hundred louis d'or which I put in the good aunt's hands; she had never seen so much money.

'I would be out of my senses, madame, if I refused my niece her fortune. I give her over to you, and I hope that you will never abandon her.'

The bargain struck, she returned to Bourges and told the company that she had no more worries over her niece, and that the Comtesse was taking charge of her. It was a great loss for them, but such is the fate of provincial actors, as soon as one or two become good, they leave and go to Paris.

Indeed du Rosan followed this very path shortly after the same tour. Floridor knew his talent and had been pressing him for six months to go to Paris. He was the head of his own troupe and he adored little Roselie, whom he foresaw would one day be a good actress. That had kept him back, but once he saw that I had taken charge of the girl he hesitated no more and went to present himself at the Hôtel de Bourgogne, where he was received with acclaim by the public.

As soon as the actors had left I returned to my house and hardly ever went to Bourges again. I had my Roselie with me. I loved her dearly, and the Comtesse des Goutes was far away with her husband.

I thought of her no more. A married woman meant nothing to me; right from the beginning the tie of wedlock dispelled her charms. The curé and the Chevalier d'Hanecourt kept us company; the Chevalier had resigned himself like a sensible man and accepted that he was to be merely one of my friends.

I treated Roselie very differently from a simple actress. I had most becoming clothes made for her and sent four of my diamond crisping-pins to Paris where they were exchanged for some lovely earrings which I gave to her. I took her with me everywhere when I went calling in the neighbourhood, and her beauty and modest demeanour charmed everyone.

I took it into my head to go hunting and dressed in a riding habit. I had Roselie dressed in the same way and found her so attractive with a peruke and a hat that I gradually made her dress entirely *en garçon*. She made a pretty cavalier and I seemed to love her more like that. I called her my little husband and everywhere we went she was known as 'the little Comte' or Monsieur Comtin; she acted as my squire.

Eventually I grew tired of seeing her in a peruke and I had her hair cut a little shorter. She had a well-shaped head, so it made her even prettier; perukes make young people look old.

This was a harmless amusement which lasted seven or eight months, but unhappily Monsieur Comtin began to feel sick, she lost her appetite and adopted the bad habit of vomiting every morning.

I suspected what had happened and made her wear her girl's clothes again, as being more proper to her present condition and more suitable for concealing it. I made her wear long, trailing, waistless *robes de chambre,* and gave out that she was unwell; her migraines and colics helped us in this deception.

The poor child often cried but I consoled her by assuring her that I would never abandon her. She confessed to me that she had neither father nor mother and did not know her origin, that her aunt was one in name only who had taken her in out of affection when she was four years old. I ceased to wonder that the so-called aunt had yielded her up to me so readily.

At the end of five or six months I saw clearly that the whole district would soon discover the truth and that there would be a scandal. Loving her as much as I did, I decided to place her in the hands of those skilled persons who could cure her of this malady, which was not dangerous, provided one did not worsen it in trying to conceal it.

We had to go to Paris where it is easy to hide oneself. I asked the curé to keep an eye on my house and I left in my carriage with Roselie, Bouju and his wife, my cook riding. I had instructed Monsieur Acarel to rent a house for me with a nice garden in the faubourg Saint-Antoine. I determined to go little into the town until the girl was cured.

As soon as I arrived I lodged Roselie with a midwife who took great care of her. I went to see her every day and gave her little presents to cheer her. I thought only of her. I thought neither of myself nor of dressing myself up. I wore modest clothes, always a coif, and never put on ear pendants or patches.

Eventually Roselie was delivered of a baby girl, whom I had well brought-up, and when she was sixteen I married her to a gentleman with an income of five or six thousand livres; she is quite happy. Her mother, at the end of six weeks, had so recovered her looks that she was more lovely than ever, and then I thought once more of my own beauty. I adorned myself and went to the theatre with two ladies who were neighbours. Roselie shone like a little star, but she was quite amazed, as was I, when we saw du Rosan on the stage playing the part of Maxime in *Cinna.*

He recognized us at once and came to see us in our box. He was overcome with joy and I could see that Roselie was by no means displeased. I told him where I was staying and gave him leave to come and see me. We saw him the very next day, and he never stopped talking of how beautiful the girl was; his passion was re-awakened.

'Madame,' he said to me, 'I have made my fortune. I still have only a half-share but I shall soon have the whole sum : an income of eight thousand livres. I shall marry Roselie, if you are willing to give her to me, and I am confident that with her looks, if she has not forgotten how to declaim verse, I shall have her accepted into the company.'

I replied that I would speak to her about it and asked him to come back in three or four days.

I spoke to her the same night, embracing her with all my heart. 'There it is,' I said, weeping, 'if you want to leave me.'

She said quite coldly that she would do everything I wished.

I did not like this, and resolved to have her married. The next day I made her sleep in a separate room, which upset her, for she thought I was angry. When everyone was in bed, she sought me in my bed and asked a hundred times for my forgiveness.

'Oh, madame,' she said, 'if I were to marry would you love me no more?'

'No, dear child,' I told her, 'a married woman should love only her husband.'

She burst into tears and embraced me so tenderly that I forgave her and imagined myself back at Crespon.

Du Rosan returned and pleaded his suit with warmth. I told him that as Roselie had nothing of her own it was essential, before anything else, that she should be accepted into the company.

'No, madame,' he retorted like a man infatuated, 'I ask for nothing. She is a little treasure-house in herself.'

I paid no attention to him and told him that I would go to the theatre the next day, that Roselie would be in my box, strikingly well-dressed, that he would remark on her to his colleagues, and that after the performance they would all come to invite me to step on to the stage, when the audience had left, to repeat some verse with the girl.

My instructions were carried out; they played *Le Menteur*.[54] Floridor, after the performance, escorted us onto the stage and to enjoy myself I enacted with the girl some scenes from *Polyeucte* which we had played together more than a hundred times.

The cast was in ecstacies and wanted to accept Roselie without another trial, but I opposed this.

'You must', I told them, 'consult the public. Advertise that she will play five or six times and then you will know.'

Du Rosan thought this far too long, but I thought it quite

short enough. The day after the marriage I would have to re-
nounce for ever the one I loved. Nevertheless I had determined
on it and I did not want to impede the progress of my dear child;
I had also noticed that she did not dislike du Rosan.

She played to the public on the stage of the Théâtre de
Bourgogne, and from the first appearance the *parterre* silenced
her with their applause. The actors accepted her formally and
gave her, on joining, a half-share.

She had no theatrical clothes and these were very expensive,
so I gave her a thousand écus to obtain them, and du Rosan also
gave her as much. He began to press for the marriage. I continued to put it off; sometimes it was clothes I had to obtain for
her, sometimes linen. I wanted the wedding to take place in my
house.

At last the fatal day came. Roselie was married and from that
day forward I did not lay a finger on her. The wedding was at
my expense and I showered her with little presents. At Crespon
I had already given her earrings worth four thousand francs.

As soon as the girl was married my thoughts turned exclusively
to myself and the longing to be a beautiful woman once more
became a passion. I had made the most beautiful clothes and
wore again my fine ear pendants which had lain neglected for
three months; ribbons, patches, coquettish manners, little affectations, nothing was forgotten. I was only twenty-three, I thought
myself still lovable and I wanted to be loved.

I went to the theatres and all the *promenades publiques*. Eventually I made so many appearances that many people recognized
me and followed me to learn where I was living.

My kinsmen were appalled that I should have resumed a
character which had been forgiven before only because of my
extreme youth. They came to see me and talked to me so
seriously about it that I decided to give up such trifling, and to
that end I departed to travel in Italy. One passion drives out
another; I gave myself to gambling in Venice, I won good sums
of money, but more than lost them afterwards.

The passion for gambling has obsessed me and has upset my life. I would have been happier if I had always made myself up as a beauty, even when I was ugly! Ridicule is preferable to poverty.

Part Two

INTRODUCTION

This is a curious and charming story, the authorship of which is not absolutely certain. The subject, although by no means indecently treated, is strange, to say the least, although certain contemporary social and literary fashions would make it unexceptionable to its original seventeenth-century readers. Bi-sexuality was notorious: Monsieur the King's brother, Lully, the Vendômes, the Comtesses de Baisson and Muret were examples, quite apart from the notorious Maupin who was not in the same caste. *L'Astrée* by Honoré d'Urfé, published in the first decade of the eighteenth century, and *La Nouvelle Astrée,* an abridged version by Choisy, were popular and dealt with a young man who, in order to marry the shepherdess he loved, pretended to be a woman, invading exclusively feminine rites in this guise. Mademoiselle Héritier de Villandon, a most austere writer, had as her favourite story, *Marmoiseau,* in which the heroine has to live as a young man.

The *Marquise-Marquis de Banneville* first appeared in the *Mercure Galant* in February 1695, and was reprinted in the *Mercure* in August and September 1696 in a version three times as long. The *Mercure Galant* was founded in 1672 by Donneau de Vizé, a writer of farces and vaudeville, and after spasmodic appearances it was published every month from 1698, becoming the *Mercure de France* in 1724. Appropriately, it was in the *Mercure de France* of 1 February, 1928 that a detailed and convincing argument was propounded by Madame Jeanne Roche-Mazon to the effect that the story was written by two hands, namely Charles Perrault, whose fairy stories everyone has read, and the Abbé de Choisy.

In the original version of 1695, Sionad and the Comtesse d'Alettef were easily identifiable as Monsieur, the King's brother, and Madame de La Fayette, who had died in 1693. (Sionad is an anagram of Adonis, and d'Alettef of La F... ette.) That this must have caused some feelings of outrage is suggested by the fact that in the new version their characters were modified: Sionad became a nineteen-year-old foreign *seigneur*, *'aussi beau que vaillant, aussi aimable parmi les Dames qu'il est fier parmi les soldats'*; d'Alettef, spelt d'Aletref or d'Altref, was the wife of an ambassador, the mother of a twelve-year-old daughter and no longer of doubtful reputation. The 1696 Marquise had a taste for fairy stories and mentioned that she knew the name of the young man who had written *La Belle au Bois Dormant,* despite the fact that when that story had appeared in the *Mercure* in February of the same year, it was stated that it was by the same *Dame* who had written the 1695 *Marquise.* This device was clearly to let Perrault off the hook so that, three months later, he could publish his *Contes* with a dedication to Mademoiselle, the King's cousin.

The text has certain signs which might indicate Perrault as the author. The ball scene in his *Cendrillon* and that in the *Marquise-Marquis* have much in common, such as the total silence when the couple danced, so complete that the *violons* could hear themselves. Untypical of Choisy are the passages where, when the little Marquise learns her true sex, she worries and talks of duty, a moral stance quite foreign to Choisy's nature, as we have seen it in his memoirs. It is evident from the introduction to the story that the purported author was the little Marquise herself, and it might be considered odd that Perrault should have allowed himself to be passed off as a woman. On the other hand, he was a supporter of blue-stockings and defended them against Boileau, so it might have pleased his fancy.

There are, however, considerations strongly in favour of Choisy as the author. There are the clear indications in the *Fragments* such as the mention of the Marquise de Banneville in the third fragment, where Choisy significantly confuses his genders, writing:

106

Je ne doute point, Madame, que l'histoire de la Marquise de Banneville ne vous ait fait plaisir; j'ay été ravie de me voir en quelque façon autorisé par l'exemple d'une personne si aimable, with *ravie* (feminine) and *autorisé* (masculine). Choisy's upbringing corresponds closely to that of the little Marquise: both delighted in the details of feminine attire; other women liked kissing both of them when they were dressed as women. There is the resemblance between Monsieur's Ball, attended by Choisy, and that of Prince Sionad (Sionad of course being Monsieur); the similarity in the little favours the Marquise granted to the Marquis de Bercour and those Choisy granted to his suitors when he was an actress in Bordeaux; the similarity between Mme de La Fayette's advice to Choisy and the comment made by Mme d'Alettef on de Bercour (*d'Alettef* being an anagram of *La F...ette*); the likeness between the nuptial bedding of the Marquise and that of Choisy with his 'little husband'; and even the similar haircuts of Choisy and de Bercour, both having it styled to display their earrings.

Perrault could not have borrowed all this from the *Fragments* which were not published and probably not even written at the time. But why should Donneau de Vizé attribute such a bizarre work as *Banneville* to one of his most successful and popular authors if he had not written it?

Perrault and Choisy may not have moved in the same social circles, but they certainly knew each other. They were both members of the Académie française, Fontanelle and Mme de Lambert were common friends, and Choisy said that certain information contained in his *Mémoires pour servir à l'histoire de Louis XIV* came from Perrault. It is possible that Choisy, who had not lost his transvestite gusto even after he had been a priest for ten years, could not resist writing the *Marquise-Marquis de Banneville*. As is was impossible for him to submit the story himself, he may have persuaded Perrault to submit it as his own, and so deceived de Vizé.

If the tale, as seems likely from the textual evidence, is part

Perrault, part Choisy, any collaboration between them probably arose from the current fashion for writing fairy tales. Perrault was the central figure of a group who exchanged fairy stories among themselves, sometimes writing on the same theme. The Marquise de Lambert was a devotee of fairy stories and a close friend of Choisy who himself produced one, *Princesse Aimonette*. Other tales, such as *Marmoisan* and *Griselidis* [55] were circulated also. Choisy may therefore have submitted some of his less scandalous reminiscences, which could have given Perrault the idea of the *Marquise-Marquis de Banneville*.

That, in compressed form, is the substance of Madame Roche-Mazon's argument. She dryly concludes with the observation that Choisy, in bed with his curl-papers and nightcap, was just as dangerous a wolf as that encountered by Perrault's Red Riding Hood. I personally consider the tale more likely to have been written by Choisy than Perrault.

The theme of the story is bizarre and, of course, quite implausible. It is hardly possible for a boy of sixteen to be unaware of his masculinity; was there no chit-chat with other girls? did the Marquise bribe the laundresses? The emotional implications are credible but not simple. The little Marquise, so strictly brought up, might well not have heard of homosexuality before she went to Paris, but there, under the wing of the Comtesse d'Alettef, she must have learnt something; she did understand sexual desire and love, inasmuch as she was acutely conscious of them and their drive was such that they overcame her initial distress at falling in love with another man. The Marquis de Bercour, on the other hand, could not have harboured any illusions, and perhaps, suddenly realizing he was a lesbian, thought himself doomed to marry a girl who was naturally heterosexual. The dénouement was, however, happy : perhaps a paradise for bi-sexual transvestites.

THE STORY OF THE
MARQUISE-MARQUIS DE BANNEVILLE

Since women are dabbling in writing and pride themselves on their fine wit, I do not wish to be the last of them to mark my zeal for my sex; but let it not be laid to my account that we are thought to be great personages in spite of all the little ways which we do not know how to shed. In fact, though we may be most proper in our works, it is there that you see Woman in a thousand aspects; lofty sentiments, whether extravagant, strained or sublime, can never hide from the discerning reader's eye a certain softness, a certain weakness which is natural to us and on which we always fall back. So we must not be given more worth than we have. To believe that a pretty young girl, brought up in the boudoir, is capable of writing like M Pellisson [56] is gross error. She will, however, have the burning warmth of her age, new turns of phrase, lively expressions, a delightful imagination. She will perhaps be more pleasing than M d'A... [57] but for exactness, substance and texture she looks to M de T..., [58] claiming only to amuse herself first in amusing her companions by her little stories.

Here then is my *coup d'essai*; you will be the judge, mesdemoiselles, because it is you to whom I appeal, but if you are over twenty I forbid you to read me. Look for something more substantial. A girl of twenty years must think of making herself a good housekeeper and she is well past the time for trifles. Moreover, do not begin to doubt what I am going to tell you. I saw it all, I knew it all, heard it all; I was an eye witness to this, and no circumstance was unnoticed by me. Some aspects will appear singular enough to you. That is exactly what gave me the wish to put them on paper; I have never thought highly of those who deal only in commonplaces. Well-worn roads are for little talents,

109

and whoever puts himself to the trouble of writing must choose a theme which stands up on its own and which, without affectation, eloquence or fancies, draws everyone's attention from the beginning. Now, on with the dance!

The Marquis de Banneville had not been married six months to a beautiful, intelligent young heiress when he was killed in the Battle of St Denis. His widow was deeply affected. They had been still in their first ardours of love, and no quarrel had clouded their happiness. She did not give way to weeping and wailing, however, and without the usual public lamentations she retired to one of her country houses to shed tears as she wished, without restraint and without ostentation. But she had hardly arrived there when she was made to recognize by certain signs that she was carrying a child. At first, the joy of seeing a little replica of the one whom she had so much loved completely possessed her. She wanted to preserve the precious remains of her dear husband and neglected nothing which would help to keep his memory fresh.

Her pregnancy was quite untroubled, but when her time drew near a thousand thoughts came to torment her. The mortal death of a man in battle came to her eyes with horrid vividness. She imagined the same fate for the child she was expecting and, being unable to bear such a sad and mournful fancy, she prayed a thousand times that Heaven would give her a girl who would be protected from such a cruel fate by her sex. She did more than that, and took it into her head to correct Nature if Nature did not respond to her wishes. To that end she made all necessary preparations and made her midwife swear that she would clearly announce the birth of a girl even if the baby should be a boy.

The matter was as easily carried through as proposed. Money can achieve everything. The Marquise was mistress in her *château*, and the news was soon spread that she had been delivered of a girl, although in fact it was a boy. The child was taken to the curé who, in all good faith, baptized it in the name of Marianne.

The wet nurse was also won over; little Marianne was reared by this wet nurse, who in due course became her governess. She was taught all that a young lady of quality should know : dancing, music, the harpsichord. Her masters had only to speak and in a moment she would grasp all they had been explaining to her. Such a great facility for learning obliged her mother to have her taught languages, history and even the new philosophy, without fear that so many sciences would intermingle in confusion in a head where everything was arranged in an unbelievably orderly manner.

What was so ravishingly wonderful was that such a fine intelligence seemed to rest in the body of an angel. When twelve years old her figure was already formed. It is true that since childhood she had been somewhat constrained by an iron bodice, to bring out her hips, and heighten her bosom, all with success, and her face, which I shall describe to you only when she first travels to Paris, was already of a perfect beauty. She lived in a wonderful innocence and had no suspicion that she could be anything but a girl. In their Province she was called *la belle Marianne*. All the neighbouring petty nobility, who looked on her as a great heiress, came to pay court to her. She listened to them all, and responded to their gallantries with much freedom of spirit.

'My heart is not for provincials,' she said one evening to her mother, 'and if I welcome them, it is because I want to be pleasing to everyone.'

'Take care, my child,' said the Marquise to her, 'you are talking like a coquette.'

'Ah, *maman*, let them be,' she replied. 'If they love me as much as they wish, what is it to you, provided that I do not love them?'

The Marquise was greatly delighted to hear her speak so, and gave her complete freedom with these young men who, for their part, never strayed from the path of respect. She knew the truth of the matter, and hence remained unconcerned. *La belle Marianne* studied until noon, and in the afternoon prepared herself for the evening.

'After giving the whole of the morning to my mind,' she would say in her agreeable way, 'it is only fair to give the afternoon to my eyes, mouth, and to my entire little person.'

And assuredly she did not begin to dress until four in the afternoon. Usually the company had assembled then and took pleasure in seeing her at her toilet. Her chambermaids arranged her hair, but she herself always added some small improvement to her coiffure. Her fair hair dropped on her shoulders in large ringlets. The sparkle of her eyes and her high colour were dazzling, and this great loveliness was sustained and animated by a thousand pretty phrases which issued at every moment from the most beautiful lips that ever were. Such young men as she had around her were in a state of adoration and she neglected nothing to excite them ever more. She herself, with a fine grace, attached pendants to her ears, of pearls, rubies or diamonds. She affixed patches, some almost imperceptible which were so tiny that one would have had to have a complexion as delicate and fine as hers for them to be perceived; but in putting them on she went to great fuss and trouble, pondering whether one or the other would best become her. Her mother was full of delight, and at every moment congratulated herself on her skill. 'He is twelve years old,' she murmured to herself. 'I would soon have had to think of sending him to the [Military] Academy, and in two years he would have been following his poor father,' and with that, transported with affection, she went to kiss her dear daughter, and allowed her to perform the little coquetries which she would have condemned in someone else's daughter.

That is how matters stood when the Marquise de Banneville was obliged to go to Paris to petition in an action at law which one of her neighbours had brought against her. She did not omit to take her daughter, and later recognized that a pretty young girl is not without her uses in the case of petitions. She first went to see the Comtesse d'Alitref, an old friend, and asked her counsel and protection for her daughter. The Comtesse was struck with Marianne's beauty and kissed her with so much delight that she returned to it several times. She undertook to look after her while her mother was occupied with her case, and promised she would not lack amusements. Marianne could not have fallen into better hands. The Comtesse, who was born for gaiety, had found a means of separating herself from an inconvenient husband. Not that he was an unworthy man, liking pleasure as much as did she, but as they did not agree on their choice of pleasures, they had the wit to wish not to constrain each other, and to follow each his own inclination. The Comtesse, although she was no longer in her first youth, still had a very lovely face; the desire for lovers had yielded to the desire for money, and play was her dominant passion. She took *la petite Marianne* everywhere and everywhere she was received with delight.

In the meantime, the Marquise de Banneville slept peacefully. She was well aware of the Comtesse's reputation, which was somewhat questionable, and she would never have entrusted a real daughter to her. However, since Marianne had been brought up with virtuous feelings and sentiments, the Marquise, in order to have some diversion herself, left her on her honour, contenting herself with telling her that she was going to find herself in a very different scene from that of their Province; that at every step she would find loving, tender and passionate suitors; that she must not be too ready to believe them and that, if she felt her heart weaken, she should come to her mother and tell her everything; that in future she would regard her as her friend rather than her daughter, and would give her the advice which she herself would take.

Marianne, whom they began to call 'the little Marquise', promised her mother that she would reveal to her all the impulses of her heart and, trusting to past experience, she believed she could brave all the gallantry of the Court of France. This was a bold undertaking thirty years ago. She had the most magnificent clothes made; the latest fashions were tried on her. The Comtesse, who presided over all this herself, took care that her hair was dressed by Mademoiselle de Canillac. She had only a child's earrings and few jewels; her mother gave her all her own, which were badly made and, without incurring great expense, means were found of making her two ear pendants of diamonds, and five or six crisping-pins to put in her hair. She needed no more for adornment. The Comtesse sent her her carriage soon after dinner and took her to the Comédie, the Opéra and to gaming houses. She was admired by everyone. Neither young girls nor women could prevent themselves bestowing caresses on her, and even the most beautiful of them felt no jealousy of the praises given to her beauty. A certain hidden charm, whose impression they felt without realizing it, drew their hearts and made them pay sincere homage to the true worth of the little Marquise; for no one could escape her influence; her imperious wit even more than her beauty caused her to make surer and more lasting conquests. At first, one was taken by the dazzling whiteness of her complexion; a rosy blush, appearing and reappearing, always took one by surprise. Her eyes were blue and none were more lively; they sparkled from beneath two heavy eyelids which made their glances more tender and languishing. The shape of her face was oval and her scarlet and slightly protruding lips produced, as soon as she spoke seriously, twenty little depressions hollowed by the Graces, and she made twenty others even more delightful when she laughed. Such a charming exterior was supported by all that a good education can add to a fine nature. The little Marquise showed a glow of modesty on her face which commanded respect. She knew how to distinguish occasions, and never went to church unless coiffed, wearing no patches and avoiding the display which the greater part of women seek.

'One must', she would say, 'pray to God at Mass and dance at a Ball, and do it whole-heartedly.'

She had spent a most agreeable life for three months when it was the time of *Carnaval*. All the princes were there, all the officers had returned from the Armies, and public entertainments were warming up on all sides. Everyone was giving a rout, and there was a Grand Ball at the Palais-Royal. The Comtesse, who was not young enough to go with her face uncovered, went there masked, and made the little Marquise one of her party. She was dressed as a Shepherdess, in a simple but becoming costume. Her hair, which fell down to her waist, was tied up in large curls with rose-coloured ribbons : neither pearls nor diamonds, but beautiful cornets. She was then only dressed as herself. She had not been dressed by anyone save herself and did not fail to attract the attention of all the company.

Her beauty was there in its triumph. The handsome Sionad was also there, dressed in women's attire, in order to compete with the fair sex, and to carry off, in the judgement of the connoisseurs, the prize of being the most beautiful of all.

When she arrived at the Ball, the Comtesse made up her mind and went to place herself behind the lovely Sionad.

'Princess,' she said to him, approaching him and presenting the little Marquise to him, 'here is a young Shepherdess who is not unworthy of a glance from you.'

Marianne drew near with respect, and was about to kiss the hem of the Prince's robe, or I should say the Princess's, but he raised her up and embraced her tenderly. 'What a beautiful child,' he cried in rapture. 'Charming features! What a smile, what delicacy! If I am not mistaken she has even more wit than beauty.'

The little Marquise had replied with no more than a modest smile, when a young Prince came to take her to dance. The respect which all the company owed to his high birth attracted everyone's eyes and attention at first, but when it was seen with what grace the young Marquise replied to him without the least confusion, her ear for music, her lightness of foot, her little jumps in tempo, her delicate smiles without malice, the fresh bloom which the exertion spread on her countenance, the whole company, as if at a concert, was reduced to silence. The *violons* [59] had the pleasure of hearing themselves play, as everyone in the room was absorbed in looking at and admiring her. The dance ended with applause, for which the Prince, well loved though he was, had only the lesser share.

The acclaim which the little Marquise had received at the assembly in the Palais-Royal redoubled the Comtesse's affection and care. She could no longer do without her, and in order to enjoy her company at her leisure she offered to give her an apartment in her house, but the mother would never consent to that. The little Marquise was nearly fourteen years old, and it was essential to the secret of her birth that no one be familiarly close to her. She was still quite ignorant of her condition and, although she had many suitors, she felt nothing towards them, thinking solely of herself and her own beauty. No one spoke to her of anything else; she drank deeply of such a delicious draught and believed herself to be the most beautiful person in the world, particularly as every day her looking-glass swore to her that it did not lie.

One day when she was at the Comédie in a box in the first tier, she noticed in the next box a handsome young man, wearing a scarlet *just-au-corps* with gold and silver embroidery, but what drew her attention more was that he had dazzling diamond rings in his ears, and three or four patches on his face. From curiosity she set herself to look at him well, and finding he had such a sweet and pleasant countenance, could not contain herself.

'Madame,' she said to the Comtesse, 'that is a handsome young man there.'

'That is true,' said the Comtesse, 'but he makes himself pretty, and that does not suit a man. Why does he not dress as a girl?'

The play continued; they ceased to converse, but the little Marquise often turned her head, and felt no more interest in the *Faux Alcibiade,*[60] which was being shown. Some days later, when she was again at the Comédie but in the third tier, the same young man who made himself so conspicuous through his extraordinary adornment, was in the second tier, and having a comfortable view of the little Marquise who was in the third, he felt all the attraction for her that she had felt for him the first

116

time, but he restrained himself less. He kept his back on the actors all the time, and could not refrain from looking up at the little Marquise, who for her part responded to him rather more than strict modesty would have allowed. In this mutual exchange of glances she felt what she had never before felt, a certain delicate and profound joy which went from the eyes into her heart, and made all the happiness there was in life. At last, when the play was over, and the audience waiting for the curtain piece, the handsome young man left his box to go and enquire the little Marquise's name. The doorkeepers, who saw her often, told it to him without persuasion and even added her place of residence. Seeing then that she was a person of quality, he resolved to make her acquaintance if he could, even without progressing further. He decided (love is ingenious) to enter the little Marquise's box abruptly, pretending he had made a mistake.

'Ah, madame,' he cried. 'I crave your pardon; I thought I was going into my own box.'

The Marquise de Banneville liked little intrigues and did not let this one escape her.

'Monsieur,' she most politely replied, 'we are very happy that you made a mistake, and when one is made as you are, one is well received everywhere.'

In that way she wanted to detain him to see him at her leisure, to examine him and his adornments, to please her daughter, whose emotion she had already noticed and, in a word, to enjoy herself harmlessly. He demurred a little and then remained in the box without putting himself in the front row. They put a hundred questions to him to which he replied with much wit and a certain charm in his voice and in his whole manner, which made him most likeable. The little Marquise asked him why he had earrings. He replied that it was from habit, and that having had his ears pierced since childhood, he always wore diamond earrings, and as for the rest, at his age little adornments were forgivable, which properly became only the fair sex.

'It all suits you well, monsieur,' said the little Marquise, blushing. 'You can wear patches and bracelets with no opposition from us. You will not be the first, for these days the young men adorn themselves like girls.'

The conversation never flagged. When the curtain piece was ended, he conducted the ladies to their carriages, and followed them in his own to the Marquise's house. There, without attempting to enter, he sent a page to present his compliments, and to say that his escort had not been necessary for them.

In the following days, they found him everywhere, at church, at the *promenades,* at public entertainments, always deferential, always respectful, bowing deeply to the little Marquise without attempting to approach or speak to her. He appeared to be concerned in only one thing, and devoted all his time to it. At last, at the end of three weeks, a *conseiller au Parlement,*[61] the Marquise de Banneville's brother, came one morning to propose that she receive a visit from the Marquis de Bercour, his good friend and neighbour. He assured her that he was an excellent man and brought him in the afternoon. The Marquis had the most beautiful head of hair, black, with natural waves falling into thick curls. It was cut in line with the ears so as to show his diamond earrings, to each of which he had that day affixed a small pearl pendant. A mere two or three patches drew attention to his lovely skin.

'Ah, brother,' said the Marquise, 'is this the Marquis de Bercour?'

'Yes, madame,' replied the Marquis, 'who cannot live much longer without seeing her who is the most beautiful in the world.'

In saying these words, he turned towards the little Marquise, who was beside herself with joy. They sat down, they talked of the news, amusements, of new books. The little Marquise could sustain all kinds of conversation, and they all soon became easy with each other. The old *conseiller* was the first to go. The Marquis remained as long as he could and was the last to leave. Thereafter, he never failed to come to pay court to the one he loved, and always prepared everything perfectly. Summer had

arrived and when they went for an excursion to Vincennes or the
Bois de Boulogne, they would find at an appointed place under
the cool of the trees a magnificent collation, which seemed to
have been brought by magic; violins today, hautboys tomorrow.
The Marquis seemed to have given no orders, but for all that it
was obvious that it all came from him. They were, however some
days without guessing who had sent a magnificent present to the
little Marquise. One morning a carrier brought a chest to her
house from, he said, the Comtesse d'Alettef. They opened it
eagerly. It was with great delight that they found therein gloves,
scented waters, pomades, perfumed oils, gold cases, little toilet
boxes, over a dozen different kinds of snuff boxes, and innumer-
able other treasures. The little Marquise thanked the Comtesse,
who did not know what she meant. In the end she guessed, but
her heart reproached her more than once for not having guessed
at first.

Through all these little attentions the Marquis hastened his
suit. The little Marquise was acutely sensible of this.

'Madame,' she said to her mother with an admirable frank-
ness, 'I no longer know where I am. Once I wanted to be
beautiful in everyone's eyes and now I want to be so only in the
eyes of the Marquis. I used to like Balls, Plays, Receptions, places
where there was much life and noise; but I care for none of that
now. To be alone and think of him whom I love, that is the
pleasure of my life. To whisper : he will come soon; perhaps he
will tell me that he loves me; because, madame, although he has
not yet said it to me – his lips have not yet uttered those lovely
words "I love you !" – it is true that his eyes and deeds have told
me that a hundred times.'

'My child,' replied the Marquise, 'I am deeply sorry for you.
Before you saw the Marquis, you were happy; everyone delighted
you, everyone loved you, and you loved only yourself, your own
person, your beauty. The desire to please was your whole desire,
and you were pleasing. Why change such a sweet life? Believe
me, my dear child, do not dream of taking advantage of the

attraction which nature has given you. Be beautiful, you have known this delight; is there any other like it? Draw all glances to yourself and the yearnings of all hearts, be charming wherever you may be, hear without cease the praises from people who are not flatterers. To be loved by all, but to love only oneself; that, my daughter, is the supreme happiness, and you can enjoy it for a long time. But you must not abdicate your throne to become a slave, you must resist the first attachment which allures you in spite of yourself. You command now, but very soon you will obey. Men are deceivers. The Marquis loves you today, tomorrow he will love another.'

'He could not love me more,' said the little Marquise. 'How could he love another?' And then she burst into tears.

Her mother, who loved her tenderly, tried to comfort her, and comforted her in fact by telling her that the Marquis was expected. She had her arrangements to protect, and they were important; and the love which was developing caused her distress. 'What will develop from all this?' she said to herself. 'What strange outcome? If the Marquis declares himself, if he summons up his courage, one could refuse him nothing. But,' she replied to herself, 'the little Marquise has been well brought up. She is sensible and at the most will permit only such trifling favours which mean nothing and which will leave them both in a state of ignorance which is absolutely essential for their happiness.' They were talking to each other in this way, when they were informed that the Marquis had sent them a dozen young partridges, and that he was at the door, unwilling to enter because he was returning from hunting.

'But he must come in,' cried the little Marquise. 'He must come in, we want to see him in his informal dress.'

He entered a moment later and gave his apologies for his powder marks, sunburn and a disordered peruke.

'No, no,' said the Marquise, 'do not deceive yourself, we would rather see you in a riding habit than wearing ear pendants.'

120

'If that is so, Madame,' he replied, 'you shall see me soon as a fire-raiser.'

He remained standing, as if to take his leave, but they made him sit down, and the mother, the good mother, told them to talk together while she went to write in her private room. The *femmes de chambre,* who were worldly wise, went into the *garderobe,* [62] and the lovers remained on their own. They did not speak for some time. The little Marquise, still full of emotion from what she had said to her mother, hardly dared to raise her eyes and the Marquis, even more bashful, looked at her and sighed. This silence was not lacking in tenderness. Long looks and uncontrollable sighs were a kind of speech to them, which well suited the lovers, and their shared embarrassment seemed a sign of their hinted love. The little Marquise was the first to rouse herself.

'You are dreaming, Marquis,' she said. 'Is it your sport which makes you dream?'

'Ah, beautiful Marquise,' said the Marquis, 'sportsmen are happy, they do not fall in love.'

'Why do you say that, Marquis?' she replied. 'Is loving such a great ill?'

'Madame, it is the greatest good in the world,' he answered, 'but when one loves on one's own, it is the greatest of all ills. I love, and I am not loved; I love the most lovable person there is. Venus herself would not presume to put herself before her. She is insensitive, she sees, she hears me, but she remains cruelly silent. With such harshness, can I doubt my fate?'

In saying these last words, the Marquis went on his knees before the little Marquise, who let him stay, and he kissed her beautiful hands without resistance from her. Her eyes were lowered, and heavy tears ran from them.

'You are weeping, beautiful Marquise,' he said. 'You are weeping and I am the cause. My love constrains you and you are weeping.'

'Ah! Marquis,' she answered with a deep sigh, 'one weeps

121

from joy as well as sadness, and I have never been in such delight.'

She said no more and, holding out her arms to her beloved Marquis, granted him those favours which she would have refused to all the kings on earth. Their caresses took the place of protestations of love. In the little Marquise's lips the Marquis found a willingness which her eyes had hidden from him, and this conversation would have lasted longer if her mother had not come from her room. She found each of them crying and laughing at the same time, and she wondered if there had ever been such tears to wipe away.

The Marquis at once rose to take his leave, but the mother in a most friendly manner, said to him:

'But do you not want to eat your partridges, monsieur?'

He needed little pressing. The thing that he wanted more than anything was to be accepted familiarly in the house. He stayed, in hunting dress as he was, and had the tender delight of seeing the one he loved eat. To see, close to, rose pink lips which opened to show gums of coral and teeth of alabaster, which opened and closed with the speed which is natural to all actions of the young; to see a lovely face in all the animation of its movements, giving a delight in their repetition, and to enjoy the same pleasure at the same time, that is what Love grants only to his favoured ones.

After that happy day, the Marquis supped there every evening. It was a regular affair, and the little Marquise's suitors, who till then had had no cause for jealousy amongst each other, took it as settled. The choice had been made, and each one admitted that beauty and vanity, however powerful they might be, were not strong enough to protect a heart against love. The Comte d' ——, who had been most ardent, strongly felt that he was being sneered at for his passion. He was handsome, well built, courageous, a soldier, and could not endure the little Marquise giving her hand to the Marquis de Bercour, whom he regarded as greatly inferior to himself in every way. He determined to pick a quarrel with him and thus to dishonour him, believing him too beautiful and too effeminate to dare to measure swords against him; but he was most taken aback when, at the first words he spoke to him at the gate of the Tuileries, he saw the Marquis, sword in hand, thrust at him relentlessly. They fought strongly, and were separated by their friends.

This adventure pleased the little Marquise greatly. It gave a war-like air to her lover whom she had till then thought would shake at the thought of combat. She saw clearly that her beauty and her attractions would bring the Marquis similar embroilments almost every day, and one evening she said to him :

'Marquis, we must put an end to all jealousy and silence the expostulators. We love each other, and we shall always love each other. We must be tied with those knots which are never broken during our lifetime.'

'Ah! beautiful Marquise,' he said, 'of what are you thinking? Are you weary of our happiness? Marriage is usually the end of delight. Let us stay as we are. As for myself, I am content with the favours you grant me. I would not ask you for more.'

'But I,' replied the little Marquise, 'I am not content; I feel that there is something lacking in our happiness, and that perhaps we shall find it when you are everything to me, and I everything to you.'

'It would not be fair,' the Marquis answered, 'for you to marry one who has only a younger son's fortune, who has squandered the best part of what he had, and whom you know only from his appearance, which is often deceptive.'

'And that is what I love,' she interrupted. 'I am delighted to have enough for us both, and most happy to show you that I am attracted only by your attractions.'

So they were, when the Marquise de Banneville interrupted them. She had just dismissed her men of affairs and thought she would revive her spirits in the cheerfulness of the young ones, but she found them deeply serious. The Marquis had been most upset by the proposal the little Marquise had made to him. She was, according to all appearances, an excellent match for him, but he had his private reasons which opposed it, and which he believed to be insurmountable. The little Marquise on her side was a little piqued to have made such a great advance to no avail, but she soon recovered, and thought that the Marquis had not accepted her proposal out of respect for her, or that he wished to prove his fidelity. This thought made her determine to speak to her mother about it, which she did the next day.

No one was ever more astonished than the Marquise de Banneville, when her daughter talked to her of marrying. She was sixteen and no longer a child. Her eyes had still not been opened to her true condition, and her mother greatly hoped that they never would be. She took care not to consent to her marrying; but to unveil the truth to her would be a harsh cure both for her and for him. She determined not to do it except as a last resort, and in the meantime to bring the proposed marriage to the Marquis to nought or at least postpone it. He was in agreement with her on this, but the little Marquise, who was strong in her desires, begged, implored, wept and used every possible means to sway her mother, having no doubts about her lover, who had not the temerity to oppose her with the same steadfastness. In the end she was so insistent, that her mother said these words to her :

'You have forced my hand, dear child, and it is against my will that I am going to reveal to you what I wished to keep hidden from you, even at the price of my life. I loved your poor father, and when I so unhappily lost him, the fear of a similar ill fate coming to you made me passionately wish to have a girl. I was not so fortunate; I gave birth to a boy, and had him brought up as a daughter. His sweetness, his loving nature, his beauty all contributed to my plan. I have a son and everyone believes that I have a daughter.'

'Oh, madame,' cried the little Marquise, 'could it be possible that I am....'

'Yes, my child,' her mother said, kissing her. 'You are a boy. I see how greatly this news affects you. Habit has given you a different nature. You are accustomed to a life far different from that which you would have led. I thought of making you happy and I would never have revealed so melancholy a truth if your persistency over the Marquis had not obliged me to do so. See now, without me, what you were going to do, to what you were going to expose yourself, and what scandal you were going to give to the public.'

Instead of replying, the little Marquise merely wept, and her mother vainly said to her:

'But, my child, continue to live in the same way. Always be the beautiful little Marquise, loved and adored by all who see her. Love your handsome Marquis, if you wish, but do not dream of marrying him.'

'Alas,' she cried through her tears, 'he does not ask more; he is in despair when I speak of our marrying. Could he know of my secret? If I believed that, dear mother, I would go and hide myself at ends of the earth, if he knew it.' On that a flood of tears. 'Alas, poor little Marquise,' she added, 'what are you going to do? Will you now dare to show yourself and make yourself beautiful? But what have you said, what have you done, how can you give a name to those favours which you granted to the Marquis? Blush, unhappy girl, blush. Ah! nature is blind not to have warned me of my duty. Alas! I acted in good faith, but now I understand, I must conduct myself quite differently in future, and in spite of him whom I love, I must do what I should do.'

She was uttering these words with determination, when it was announced that the Marquis was at the door of the antechamber. He entered with a happy air, and was astounded to see mother and daughter with lowered eyes and in tears. The mother, without waiting for him to speak, rose and went into her private room, and left him on his own. Then he took courage:

'What is it, beautiful Marquise?' he said, dropping to his knees. 'You have some sorrow – cannot you share it with your friends? You do not even look at me! Is it then I who have made you shed tears, and should I be to blame without knowing it?'

The little Marquise looked at him and dissolved into tears.

'No, no,' she cried, 'no, that is impossible, and if it were true I should not feel what I do feel. Nature is wise, and her workings have reasons.'

The Marquis did not know what all this meant. He was asking for an explanation when the mother, being a little restored, came from her room and went to her daughter's rescue.

'You see her,' she said to the Marquis, 'you see her quite beside herself. It is my fault. In spite of me she had her fortune told, and they said she would never marry the one she loved; that has upset her, *monsieur le Marquis,* and you now know the reason.'

'As for me, madame,' he replied, 'that does not trouble me at all. May she remain always as she is, and for me I ask only to see her; I should be most happy if she would grant me the title of the first among her friends.'

The conversation did not last long. Their minds were too troubled and some time was needed to put them back to their usual equilibrium; but it came so perfectly that in a week there was no sign of any upset. The Marquis's presence, his charm, his endearments obliterated all that her mother had told her of her condition from the little Marquise's mind. She believed it no more or did not wish to believe it; her delight took her from reflecting on it. She spent her life in the usual way with her lover, and felt her passion increase with such violence that the thought of an eternal union came to torment her again. 'Yes,' she said to herself, 'he will not renegue and he will never leave me.' She had determined to speak of it again when her mother fell ill from such a grave illness that after three days they despaired of her recovery. She made her will, and sent for her brother, the *conseiller,* whom she made guardian of the little Marquise. He was her uncle and her heir, because all the property came from the mother. She told him confidentially of the truth of her daughter's birth, begging him to take heed of it and to let her live in her innocent happiness which harmed no one, and which, making her unable to be married, assured a large inheritance to his children.

126

The good *conseiller* learnt this news with great joy, and saw his sister die without shedding a tear. The thirty thousand livres income which she left to the little Marquise seemed destined for his children, and he had only to gratify his so-called niece's obstinacy. He did it beautifully, telling her that he would be as a mother to her, and that he had no wish to be her guardian, except nominally.

These understanding ways gave a little comfort to the little Marquise, who was truly sorrowful, but the sight of her beloved Marquis comforted her even more. She saw herself as absolute master of her fate, and thought only of sharing it with the one she loved. Six months of formal mourning passed, and then all pleasures came crowding back to the little Marquise. She went often to Balls, to the Comédie, to the Opéra, and always with the same escort. The Marquis never left her and all the other suitors, seeing clearly that it was a settled affair, retired from the contest. They lived happily, and perhaps would not have thought of anything else if malicious tongues could have left them in peace. Everywhere it was said that the little Marquise was indeed beautiful, but that since the death of her mother she had not kept within bounds; that she was seen everywhere with the Marquis; that her house was almost his; that he supped there every evening, and did not leave until midnight. Her best friends found fault with her; anonymous letters were written to her; her uncle was told of it, and he spoke to her. In the end, things went so far that the little Marquise took up her first notion, again, and to silence everybody, she resolved to marry the Marquis. She spoke to him of it most forcibly; even so, he resisted and consented to the idea only on the condition that the marriage would be merely for the public eye, and that they would live together as brother and sister, there being no other means, he said, of loving each other for ever. The little Marquise [63] willingly agreed to this condition. What her mother had told her came sometimes into her mind. She spoke of her intentions to her uncle, who at first depicted to her the thorns and thistles of wedlock and ended by

127

giving his consent. In his heart he was delighted. Therefrom he saw an income of thirty thousand livres assured to his family, and had no fear of his niece having children by the Marquis de Bercour. If she did not marry, her fantasy of being a girl could change in the course of years with her beauty, which would inevitably fade. So the marriage was arranged. Clothes were made, and the ceremony took place at the good uncle's house, who, as guardian, wanted to give the wedding feast.

Never had the little Marquise appeared so beautiful as on that day. She wore a gown of black velvet covered with precious stones, and diamond ear pendants. The Comtesse d'Alittref, who always loved her, escorted her to the church, where the Marquis waited in a black velvet cloak bedecked with gold lace, curled, powdered, with earrings and patches, so much adorned that his best friends could not forgive him for such devotion to personal display. They were joined together for ever, and everyone gave them a thousand blessings. In the evening, the festivities were magnificent; the King's music and the *violons* were there. At last the fateful hour arrived. Relatives and friends put them together in the nuptial bed and embraced them, the men laughing, and some good old aunts weeping.

It was then that the little Marquise was most astonished to see her lover's coldness and indifference. He was at the other side of the bed, sighing and crying. She moved half way to him, without his seeming to notice it. In the end, unable to bear such wretchedness any longer :

'What have I done to you, Marquis?' she said. 'Don't you love me any more? Say something, or you will see me die.'

'Alas, madame,' said the Marquis to her, 'what I said to you was right; we were living happily, you loved me and you are going to hate me; I have deceived you, come near and see.'

At the same time he took her hand and placed it on the most lovely bosom.

'You see,' he added, dissolving into tears, 'you see that I am useless to you, because I am a woman as you are.'

Who could describe the surprise and joy of the little Marquise? At that moment she had no doubts that she was a boy, throwing herself into the arms of her beloved Marquis, she was the cause of the same surprise and joy to him. Peace was soon made. They wondered at their fate, which had guided them so happily, and made a thousand protestations of eternal fidelity.

'For myself,' said the little Marquise, 'I am so accustomed to being a girl that I want to remain a woman all my life. How could I wear a man's hat?'

'As for me,' said the Marquis, 'I have had my sword in my hand more than once without being ill-at-ease, and I shall tell you my story one day. So let us remain as we are. Rejoice, beautiful Marquise, in all the charms of your sex, and I shall enjoy all the freedom of mine.'

The day after the wedding they received the usual compliments, and a week later they left for the province where they are still living in one of their châteaux. The Uncle will have to go to see them, and he will be most surprised to see an infant boy born of such a marriage, who will take from him all hope of a great inheritance.

NOTES

Part One

INTRODUCTION

1 *surintendant des finances*: Financial Administrator-General.

2 *conseiller d'état*: Privy Councillor.

3 *noblesse de robe*: titles granted to those who had served in senior judicial and administrative positions.

4 *maître des requêtes*: the senior official responsible to the Privy Council.

5 *intendants*: powerful functionaries, created by Richelieu, who acted in their allotted territories under the King's authority, controlling fiscal, judicial and police administration.

6 *précieuses*: *l'esprit précieuse* was originally an attempt at elegance in speech and writing, pursuing clarity and avoiding clumsiness and coarseness of expression. Unfortunately, the language of the *précieuses* often became so elaborate and artificial that it was both incomprehensible and ridiculous.

7 *tentative*: a public oral examination of candidates for the Bachelor of Theology degree.

8 *trésorier général*: Chief Treasurer. France was divided into twenty-one districts (*généralités*). In each one a board of ten *trésoriers de France* drew up an annual budget.

9 *conclaviste*: an appointment similar to that of aide-de-camp or judge's marshal.

10 Choisy's transvestism inspired a novel, *Les aventures du Chevalier de Faublas,* by Louvet, published in 1789. Louvet's hero was a young man who used drag as a means of seducing women, rather than as an enjoyable activity in itself. *Faublas* gave rise to another novel, *Trois Faublas de ce temps-là,* by Servin, published in 1803. The three Faublas were the Comte de Guiche, Ferdinand, the painter, and Choisy. A novel on Choisy himself, *Mademoiselle de Choisy,* by Roger de Beauvoir, was published in 1848. In it Choisy uses his trans-

vestite skill as a spy in Court intrigues and appears as a genuine hero, full of valour and self-sacrifice.

THE TRANSVESTITE MEMOIRS

I

11 *robes de chambre*: long, loose housecoats with a short train, made from magnificent materials. They were intended for indoor wear; that Choisy wore them out of doors was probably his own whim.

12 *patches*: These beauty spots (as we would call them) are said to have originated from the need to conceal pockmarks or other facial blemishes. Patches were made from silk, satin, velvet or any other suitable material, gummed on one side. The wearer dipped them in water to make them adhere. They were not always round but could be cut in star, half-moon and other shapes. The Duchess of Newcastle wore one which was a miniature silhouette of a coach and horses. The fashion began about 1650 and lasted until the end of the century.

13 *fontange*: Mademoiselle de Fontanges was for two years (1679-81) the mistress of Louis XIV. It is said that when she was out riding one day her hat was swept away by the branches of a tree and to control her hair she tied it up in a ribbon. The style became immediately fashionable; it grew more extravagantly elaborate until it became a wired 'duck's tail' of material projecting over the forehead. Towards the end of the century Lady Sandwich appeared at the French Court in a simple, low coiffure and this killed the fashion. Choisy here anticipates the fashion by some twenty years.

14 *just-au-corps*: a long sleeveless jerkin, worn, as the name implies, close to the body. They could be made from any material, from leather to silk.

15 *moiré*: watered silk.

16 Choisy's dates are confused here. The *Mercure Galant* was first published in 1672, irregularly to begin with but monthly from 1678. Even if Choisy refers to a very early edition of the paper, it would bring us to 1672 by which time he had abandoned his transvestite seductions, spent some time in Italy gambling away his money and was in that year at the Passage of the Rhine.

17 Henri Harault de l'Hospital, sieur de Belesbat.

18 *steenkirk*: Choisy again anticipates a fashion dating from the Battle of Steinkirk in 1692. The French were surprised by the English and their allies and, having no time to adjust their cravats, tied them loosely round their necks. After the French victory, the style became

fashionable and was known as a *stinquerque* in French and 'steenkirk' or 'steinkirk' in English. When worn by women it was a length of ribbon, broad or narrow, falling from the neck loosely over the bosom.

19   *cornets*: a kind of night-cap with ribbons reaching to below the shoulder. The word (*cornettes* in French) is used in the plural because it is an abbreviation for 'night bonnet with cornets'.

20   *chanteau*: literally 'slice of bread', the term used for a piece of blessed bread sent to a woman who would offer it in church the following Sunday. She carried it round, begging alms from the seated members of the congregation. It is not to be confused with the Host.

21   *échelle*: in this context a series of large or small bows of ribbon, attached from the bosom to the waist of a lady's dress, giving a ladder-like effect.

22   *mantuas*: Mantuas (corruption of French *manteaux*) were loose casual gowns worn by women.

23   *salut*: the benediction at the end of the Service of Benediction.

24   *lotteries*: popular with Louis XIV as a form of hospitality. He held them at his entertainments, taking care that his own tickets never won, Choisy, along with many others, followed the fashion, his prizes being small presents.

25   Elsewhere in the *Fragments* (p. 73) Choisy writes that coffee and chocolate were unknown and tea only beginning to be so.

26   *coif*: a close-fitting cap covering the top, back and sides of the head, worn by both sexes.

27   *de Troyes*: a French painter born at Toulouse in 1645. He died in Paris in 1730.

28   *jeudi gras*: the Thursday before Ash Wednesday.

29   *plaque*: an ornamental silver wall sconce.

30   *Marseilles corset*: probably a corset made from Marseilles silk.

31   Choisy here quotes some doggerel, not worth translating. It is full of praise for Choisy, his beauty, his generosity, his hospitality, his good works, the refrain being that 'he will have many love affairs'. There must have been other street songs which were less uncritical and it is characteristic that he recollected only those which satisfied his vanity.

II

32   *promenades publiques*: public places where people would go to be seen and to greet each other.

33   *Doctrine chrétienne*: either a church or a House of the Doctrinarians.

34   *petite ruelle*: literally a narrow lane or alley. In late seventeenth-century France it also meant both the space between a bed and a

wall, and also a salon held by a lady in her bedroom, and it was used in both these senses by the English. When a lady entertained, the company sat near her bed on the side which was called the *grande ruelle,* the side nearest the wall being the *petite ruelle.*

35 *Estrapade*: an old quarter of Paris in what is now the 5th *arondisse-ment.* The word *estrapade* meant a form of execution in which malefactors were strung up to a height and then dropped. This was repeated until the victim was dead.

36 *emplâtres*: An *emplâtre* is an adhesive covering, so presumably these were outsize patches.

37 *surintendant des bâtiments*: official in charge of public buildings.

III

38 Fragment III, though incomplete, is included in the text because of its interest and because it links with the reference to Montfleury in Fragment IV (p. 91). We can assume from this that the episodes described in Fragment III occurred just before those of Fragment IV – both end with Choisy's departure for Italy. Mondory was a distinguished actor (see note 53) and 'the little actress Mondory' may have been his daughter.

39 *the President*: a *président* was one who presided over a tribunal. In this case he was evidently a practising lawyer who was also a judge.

40 *Rotrou*: Jean de Rotrou (1609-1650) was a friend of Corneille although professionally they were rivals. *Venceslas,* a tragedy, was produced in 1647.

IV

41 *émancipation*: an arrangement by which a youth in legal minority could manage his own affairs as if he were of age.

42 *Ferdinand*: a fashionable portrait painter of the time. According to la Croix he was not Italian but Dutch.

43 *courante*: a popular dance of the period.

44 *Monsieur de Montausier*: Charles de St Maur, Marquis and later Duc de Montausier (1610-1690) was a distinguished soldier. He was made preceptor to the Dauphin in 1668. He may have been the original of Alceste in Moliere's *Le Misanthrope.*

45 *parterre*: a term used to mean both the floor of the auditorium and the audience who assembled there, who were generally rowdy and ill-behaved. Except at the Palais-Royal, where there was a series of gently-sloping narrow terraces, it was flat.

133

46 *Turin rosolio*: a sweet cordial made chiefly in Italy.

47 See note 25.

48 *Polyeucte*: a play by Corneille, first produced in 1641 or 1642. From the frequency with which it appears in the *Fragments* it appears to have been Choisy's favourite play.

49 *Chambonnière*: a French harpsichordist and composer, born in 1607. He was responsible for bringing the Couperin family to Paris in the 1650s.

50 *Carnaval*: the period between Epiphany and Ash Wednesday.

51 *Floridor*: the stage name of Josias de Saulas. He was born at Brie in the early part of the seventeenth century, the son of a German gentleman whose family had settled in France. He entered the army but soon left it for the theatre. He first appeared in Paris in 1640, joined the company at the Hôtel de Bourgogne (see note 53) three years later, and became the leading actor of his day.

52 In Paris theatrical performances were not given nightly but only three times a week.

53 *Hôtel de Bourgogne*: the *Hôtel* was originally the old residence of the Dukes of Burgundy in Paris. On the same site in the sixteenth century stood the only permanent theatre in the city. In the early seventeenth century the company was known as the *Comédiens du Roi*; it left Paris from 1622 to 1628, when the theatre was occupied by the *Comédiens du Prince d'Orange*. The principal actor of this troupe was Mondory. On the return of the *Comédiens du Roi*, he moved his troupe to the Hôtel de Marais. Molière brought his company to Paris in 1658 and, after his death, they and the best of the Marais company combined to form the company of Mazanine, later called the *Compagnie de Guénéguaud*. In 1680 these players and those from the Hôtel de Bourgogne merged, the resulting company surviving as the *Comédie-Française*.

54 *Le Menteur*: a comedy by Corneille. The plot concerns a young man who is an incorrigible romantic.

Part Two

INTRODUCTION

55 *Griselidis*: *Patient Griselda*, originally by Boccaccio, used also by Chaucer and Dekker.

THE MARQUISE-MARQUIS DE BANNEVILLE

56 *M. Pellisson*: Pellisson had been secretary to Fenquet and later wrote *Histoire de l'Académie Française,* (up to 1652), Choisy's friend, the abbé d'Olivet, completing it to 1700.

57 *M. d'A . . .* : probably the abbé Dangeau, who converted Choisy in 1683.

58 *M. de T . . .* : de Treville, a learned and grave member of the *Académie.*

59 *the violons*: a consort from the Vingt-Quatre Violons, the King's private string orchestra.

60 *Faux Alcibiade*: an allusion to Quinault's *Le Feint Alcibiade,* first produced in 1658. It's subject was appropriately sexually equivocal: Alcibiade's sister, Cleone, is a refugee in Sparta, passing herself off as her brother. Three people fall violently in love with her: a Queen, a Princess and a *cavalier,* of whom the *cavalier* finally carries her off. Quinault, together with Pellisson, Dangeau and de Treville, was well-known to Perrault and to Choisy.

61 *conseiller au Parlement*: a member of a legal body which registered and gave sanction to royal edicts. The *parlements* were divided into provinces, the most important being in Paris.

62 *garderobe*: this could be anything from a chest for storing clothes to a small ante-room, here obviously the latter.

63 *The little Marquise*: the text here has 'il'.

SELECTED BIBLIOGRAPHY

Alembert, Jean Le Royal d', *Oeuvres Philosophiques, Eloge de Choisy,* vol. 8 (Paris, 1805).

Argenson, Marquis d', *Mémoires* (Paris, 1825).

Beauvoir, Roger de, *Mademoiselle de Choisy* (Paris, 1848).

Choisy, François Timoléon, Abbé de, *Journal ou suite du voyage de Siam* (Amsterdam, 1687).

————, *La Nouvelle Astrée* (Paris, 1713).

————, *Mémoires de l'abbé de Choisy habillé en femme,* see under La Croix, Mongrédien and Percefleur.

————, *Mémoires pour servir à l'Histoire de Louis XIV,* see under Mongrédien and Michaud.

Desnoiresterres, Gustave, 'Les Originaux', *Revue Française* (Paris, 1856).

La Croix (ed.), *Mémoires de l'abbé de Choisy habillé en femme* (Paris, 1862).

Louvet de Couvray, Jean-Baptiste, *Les Aventures du Chevalier de Faublas* (Brussels, 1869).

Michaud, J. F., and J. J. F. Poujoulat (eds.), *Mémoires pour servir à l'Histoire de Louis XIV* (Paris, 1850).

Mongrédien, Georges, *Mémoires de l'abbé de Choisy, Mercure de France* (Paris, 1966).

Olivet, P. J. T. d', *Vie de M. l'abbé de Choisy* (Lausanne and Geneva, 1742).

Percefleur, Chevalier de, *Mémoires de l'abbé de Choisy habillé en femme* (Paris, 1920).

Roche-Mazon, Jeanne, 'L'Abbé de Choisy et Charles Perrault', *Mercure de France* (Paris, 1928).

Sainte-Beuve, C. A., *Causeries de Lundi,* vol. 3 (Paris, 1852).